DARTMOOR ~ SEASONS ~

Text by Elizabeth Prince
Photography by John Head

DEVON BOOKS

Produced in association with the Dartmoor National Park Authority

First published in Great Britain in 1987 by Devon Books

ISBN: 0 86114–782–0 hardback
0 86114–793–6 paperback

British Library Cataloguing-in-Publication Data
Prince, Elizabeth
Dartmoor Seasons
1. Dartmoor National Park (England)
I. Title II. Head, John
719'. 32' 0942353 SB 484. G7

Printed and bound in Great Britain by A. Wheaton & Co. Ltd.

DEVON BOOKS

Official Publisher to Devon County Council
Devon Books is a division of A. Wheaton & Co. Ltd, which represents:

Editorial, Design, Publicity, Production and Manufacturing
A. Wheaton & Co. Ltd
Hennock Road, Marsh Barton, Exeter, Devon EX2 8RP
Tel: 0392 74121; Telex 42749 (WHEATN G)
(A. Wheaton & Co. Ltd is a member of the Pergamon/B.P.C.C. Group of Companies)

Sales and Distribution
Town & Country Books, P.O. Box 31, Newton Abbot, Devon TQ12 5AQ Tel: 08047 2690.

ACKNOWLEDGEMENTS

The publishers wish to thank the following for providing photographs reproduced in this book.

John Clements: pp. 14 (lower), 26 (top & foot), 34 (lower), 35 (lower), 36 (lower), 39, 41 (lower), 43 (lower), 49 (lower right), 55 (lower), 60 (lower right), 65 (lower), 91 (upper), 93 (lower), 110 (centre), 115 (upper), 130 (upper), 132 (upper), 137 (lower left & right), 145 (lower), 147.

Dartmoor National Park Authority: pp. 26 (centre), 50 (top left), 70 (lower), 82 (upper).

Simon Ford: p. 141 (lower left).

Ian Mercer: pp. 14 (upper), 105 (centre & foot).

Paul Salmon: pp. 12, 29 (upper), 41 (upper), 44 (lower), 53, 131 (inset), 141 (right).

John Webb: p. 95.

Viv Wilson: p. 4 (lower), 21 (upper), 30 (top left), 63 (upper).

Black and white photographs are reproduced from originals in the Westcountry Studies Library.

All other photographs are by John Head.

PREFACE

This is a book about a landscape and the life within it. Perhaps more than most uplands Dartmoor varies enormously with the seasons. For this reason the photographs have been organized in the sequence in which they were taken (though over several years) from the beginning of the natural year in spring to its conclusion in winter.

The seasons are the basis for the constant renewal of nature and all living things. Most of us in the latter half of the twentieth century live in towns and cities and do not derive a living directly from the land or live particularly 'close to Nature'. Yet we still respond strongly and directly to the passage of the seasons. The coldness of the winter ('when icicles hang by the wall and Dick the Shepherd blows his nail') may be uncomfortable but is right for the time of year and therefore tolerable, even welcome. There is something fundamentally reassuring, although perhaps not consciously acknowledged, that spring, summer, autumn and winter will continue their familiar pattern no matter what our private and public griefs, follies and problems; that green buds unfailingly appear in spring and in autumn the fruits of that growth; that the vitality in the teaming animals of this planet is renewed for endless generations of each species. An Indian chief whose culture was an integral part of this natural world expressed it simply but powerfully:

> If all the beasts were gone, men would die from great loneliness of spirit, for whatever happens to the beasts also happens to the man. All things are connected. Whatever befalls the earth befalls the sons of earth.
>
> (Chief Seathl of the Suwamish tribe, in a letter to the President of the United States, 1855)

Perhaps sharing this fundamental knowledge, the poets of our own country have from earliest recorded times paid great attention to all aspects of natural life and landscape. They are particularly sensitive to the seasons and their passage. Many regretfully compare the constant renewal of the seasons with the decay and death of individual human life and love. Even by the early nineteenth century, they were conscious that humankind had become alienated from the processes of nature.

But the cycle of the seasons is ever present. The Victorian poet, Arthur Hugh Clough, marvelled at:

> This aged earth that each new spring
> Comes forth so young, so ravishing
> In summer robes for all to see,
> Of flower, and leaf, and bloomy tree,
> For all her scarlet, gold, and green,
> Fails not to keep within unseen
> That inner purpose and that force
> Which on the untiring orbit's course
> Around the sun, amidst the spheres
> Still bears her thro' the eternal years.
>
> (Arthur Hugh Clough, 'Two Moods')

The poets have always advised us to look and listen more carefully. As Vernon Watkins put it, 'A poor life this, if, full of care, We have no time to stand and stare'.

Nowadays we need to take rather more time to do this to become more in tune with the rhythm and beauty of our world and less casual about disturbing or destroying it. Gerard Manley Hopkins made a plea for one particular kind of landscape which, even when he was writing, was being diminished by the activities of man:

> What would the world be, once bereft
> Of wet and of wildness? Let them be left,
> O let them be left, wildness and wet;
> Long live the weeds and the wilderness yet.

Much of Dartmoor is 'wildness and wet' and we would indeed be bereft without it. This aspect of it and its thin rocky soil and relatively cold wet climate have prevented the wholesale 'taming' that has taken place in much of the lowlands over the centuries. Dartmoor is often referred to nowadays as the 'last great southern wilderness'. Today we value this quality highly because of its rarity and this appreciation led to its designation as a National Park in 1951.

Dartmoor was not always cherished for its 'wilderness'. It was dismissed by Camden, a sixteenth-century writer and traveller, as a 'squalid mountain' and in the following century the agricultural commentator Risdon said dispassionately that it 'was richer in the bowels than in the face thereof' (referring to its mineral wealth). But in the nineteenth-century came a change of attitude towards all wild scenery. In 1838 William Howitt, a social reformer and writer, wrote:

> If you want sternness and loneliness, you may pass into Dartmoor. There are wastes and wilds, crags of granite, views into far off districts, and the sound of waters hurrying away over their rocky beds, enough to satisfy the largest hungering and thirsting after poetical delight. I shall never forget the feelings of delicious entrancement with which I approached the outskirts of Dartmoor.
>
> (*Rural Life of England*, 1838, Vol. II, p.378)

Sabine Baring-Gould, well known for his collecting of West Country folk songs at the turn of the century wrote:

> Dartmoor. There is far finer mountain scenery elsewhere, but there can be no more bracing air, and the lone upland region possesses a something of its own – a charm hard to describe, but very real – which engages for once and for ever the affections of those who have made its acquaintance.
>
> (A *Book of Dartmoor*, 1900)

Everyone who has walked on Dartmoor will recognize that Dartmoor does indeed engage the affections and never more so than today when it is the only extensive open area in the South of England where freedom, exhilaration and peace are there for the seeking.

Part of the philosophy of English National Parks is that those whose affections are engaged in the way Baring-Gould describes are also likely to be champions against unsightly development and unnecessary 'improvement'. In presenting this book of photographs we hope to extend for its millions of visitors a perspective that is beyond the summer aspect they normally see and show the beauty and interest to be found in the 'off' seasons. Better knowledge breeds appreciation and caring

which in practical terms becomes the political will to protect a unique and precious landscape.

The photographs are not a complete record of a year on Dartmoor; they have been selected for their interest, atmosphere and beauty. But the selection includes a good cross-section of places, topics and activities. For instance, the main annual farming activities are depicted; good examples of Dartmoor's exciting prehistoric past are there; typical and particular historical built features are shown; there is every type of landscape, many kinds of habitat, a sample of characteristic wildlife and plants, and glimpses of the life and work of the 30 000 people who live today within the National Park boundary.

To see and experience the heart of the north or south plateaux you need to walk and the walking itself is of course part of the pleasure. However, as the photographs in this book show, it is not essential to be a walker to enjoy the beauty of the landscape or its detail. Through having 'an eye to appreciate' the photographer has found beauty close at hand, often within fairly easy striking distance of a road.

The book is merely a sample of the visual beauty and interest of Dartmoor. Each photograph can, after all, only capture a certain scene or event in the split-second context of a particular light, weather and season. The prettiest coombe, with its clear lively stream, warm granite boulders and heather and whortleberries bobbing in a summer breeze will in winter be a sodden depression between hills, with its stream dark and swollen, and dead-looking vegetation blown almost horizontal by a cutting east wind. The first is enchanting; the fierceness of the second is challenging. The sample is a celebration of Dartmoor's infinite variety.

The photographer's view

Dartmoor is the 'backdrop' to a Devonian's life. As a child, living near a river I felt one day that I had to set off to see where the river came from. Going up through a wooded valley I reached stone-walled fields and then the moor, broadening in all directions. Looking back was also a feast to the eye – Plymouth Sound, the Erme Valley and Mothecombe. Going further into the moor I discovered that someone had been there before – yesterday, 100 years or 1000 years before? Whatever time it was, it made an exciting discovery. It has given me great pleasure to be able to capture something of Dartmoor through a camera.

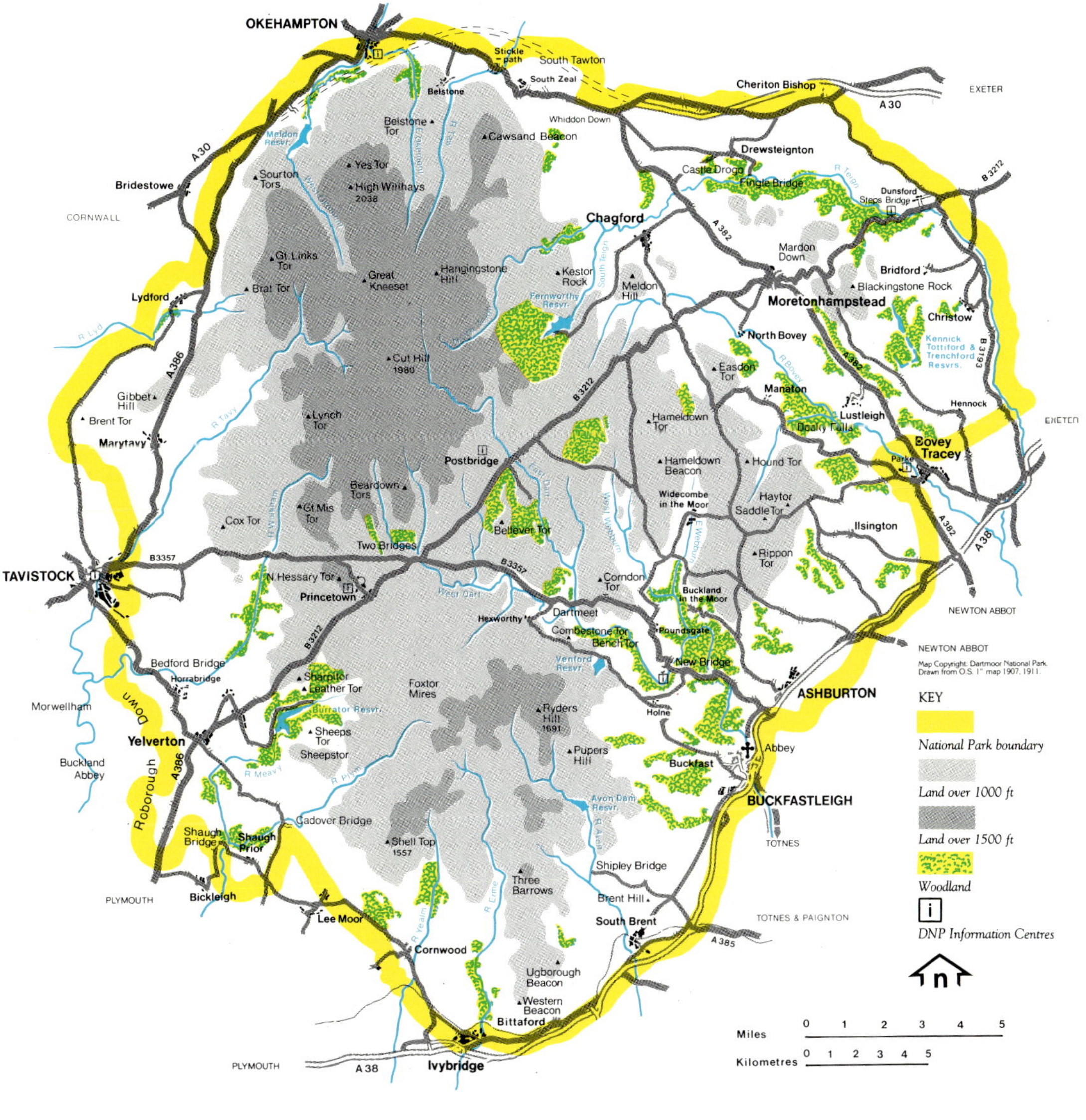

INTRODUCTION

The moor where the River Dart rises has always been a special place. Bronze Age settlers divided it meticulously between them; Britons circled it with hill-forts; Anglo-Saxons peopled all its valleys; and King John retained its heart as royal 'Forest', or hunting ground, in 1204. All Devonians – bar a few townsfolk – had rights of common grazing on it for centuries; its minerals have been exploited for longer; and for 5000 years someone, somewhere, has been tinkering with its soil, moving its boulders into walls, manipulating its water, or, having to cross it, has marked the way.

Dartmoor is now a National Park. This modern special status recognizes all those historic processes that have contributed to it through time, the need to keep many of them going, and of course the natural Dartmoor that is veiled but not obscured by them.

It is a compact 365-square-mile upland lying between the Tamar and the Exe, or, if you like, between the A30 and the A38. It is 26 miles from Okehampton to Ivybridge, and 26 miles from Brentor to Hennock. The vast bulk of Dartmoor is a granite mass with a border of baked country rock, the whole standing up out of the remnants of the slates and shales of south and mid Devon which once buried it. The molten granite was intruded, and cooled, at great depth some 250 million years ago. Since then erosion has slowly stripped all the overlaying and much surrounding rock away, creating the principle elements of the modern landscape before the last Ice Age. The original granite cracked as it cooled and cracked again as the weight of overlying rocks was removed. The cracks, well seen in all the tors, are the means by which the detail of the landscape has been etched over the last half million years. Throughout the Ice Age Dartmoor stood just outside of the extended polar ice cap. Glaciers did not move in Dartmoor valleys, but ice penetrated thousands of feet down within the granite. It sealed all those cracks at depth, and expanded in them near the surface, levering away block after block from hill top, valley side and spur end. The Tors are the result of this action, with boulder 'clitter' below them. In the brief 'Arctic' summer of each periglacial year only the surface thawed, and, as no water could seep away downwards, it swilled the whole surface, all fine particles were washed downhill, and short-lived torrents swept boulders in masses down the valleys. The French call the result a 'chaos', which aptly describes the process and the jumble of blocks.

All this ended – or paused – only 16000 years ago here in the south. Immediately plants began to recolonize the surface and soils to develop. On the high tops of Dartmoor rainfall was heavy enough to preclude effective decay of dead plant remains, so the build-up of peat began, eventually to blanket the whole of the plateau surface. From the pollen preserved in that same peat we know that forest spread right up to the edge of this blanket bog, at about 1500 feet above sea level.

Neolithic men started, and Bronze Age men almost completed, the clearance of that forest back to the steepest valley sides and thus began the whole history of man's intervention in this wildest of southern English landscapes. All the evidence is that it was slightly warmer and drier than it is now because, having cleared the trees, the inhabitants began clearing the boulders into linear piles, or rudimentary walls, to make spaces for pasturing and perhaps cultivation. By the end of the Bronze Age its people had built thousands of circular huts on Dartmoor, some in groups, some in pounds, some with square fields and some quite isolated. Their cultures demanded ceremonial stone circles, and stone rows, menhirs and burial cists. Eventually they divided large areas of land into strips and parcels by long low stone banks, now called 'reaves'. All these things still remain and, for its area, Dartmoor carries the densest collection of such artefacts in north-western Europe.

During the Iron Age, in response to a worsening climate and the formation of acid peat soils, man seems to have withdrawn to the edge of the moor, but left the remains of many hill-forts there. The Romans passed around this useless hill to north and south, and the Dark Ages were as dark here as anywhere. What is clear, however, is that Anglo-Saxon occupation in later centuries extended throughout the valleys and on to the fringes of the high moor; all but one of the villages that exist today, and some of the hamlets and isolated farmsteads, were manors at the time of the Norman Conquest. The houses they were building were longhouses and so effective was the pattern – human quarters, cross passage, cattle shippon, down the slope in that order, but all under one roof – that it persisted until the seventeenth century. Most longhouses have been adapted since, but a few remain with unaltered shippons and only slightly modified dwelling spaces.

A man fishes from the stepping stones across the River Teign, beside Rushford Mill, near Chagford, seen here in c. 1900

The Conquest cut into a period of growing population and expansion which pushed the frontiers of farming further up the slopes of Dartmoor. Medieval exploitation of farming on higher moorland is evidenced by field patterns and farmstead ruins on Holne Moor and up the West Webburn at Blackaton and Challacombe. The first written evidence of the ancient tenements of the Forest (mainly within the Dart Valley) dates from the mid thirteenth century, although it is possible that they were established long before. Following the Black Death and climatic deterioration in the fourteenth century there was an inevitable retreat from the high moor sites, and only a few have been reworked in subsequent centuries.

So, Bronze Age farmers had pushed back the woodland to its present position, innocently inventing moorland – between blanket bog and valley side – while they were at it. Saxon and medieval farmers had invested the broader valleys in a dense network of field walls, banks and lanes, and punctuated them with villages, hamlets and farmsteads. At the end of the eighteenth century the first agri-business men appeared; they drove turnpikes across the middle of the moor and strung a loose net of stone walls alongside them to create yet another farming landscape of 'newtakes', some of which are single fields of 1000 acres. These men, too, planted the shelter-belts of beech which characterize Postbridge and the West Webburn slopes.

Throughout this time another activity was making its mark within the moor. Medieval tin streamers dug over nearly every valley floor, their Tudor successors opened up vast gullies and drove adits into hillsides, and by the eighteenth century vertical shafts were being sunk. Water-wheels spun, belts whipped, rods reciprocated, bellows blew and stamps stamped; all getting, processing and shifting tin amid billowing smoke and gunpowder explosion. Around the edge of the moor lead, copper, iron and arsenic were all mined in turn, and sometimes together. Granite began to be quarried for the first time in the late eighteenth century too; there was so much lying about that quarrying was unnecessary before that. Dartmoor granite was shipped to London for Thames bridges and Nelson's Column in the early years of the nineteenth century by the new entrepreneurs. Holborn Viaduct and New Scotland Yard continued the tradition.

While all this mineral working was at its nineteenth-century height, the railways came. Between 1844 and 1849 the Exeter to Plymouth line was built; branches were extended to Moretonhampstead in 1866 and Ashburton in 1872. The line through Okehampton to Plymouth was completed in 1871, and by 1883 trains reached Princetown.

Unlike the earlier travellers, such as Camden and Celia Fiennes, who avoided the moor, locally based intrepid 'visitors' had begun to penetrate Dartmoor on foot and horseback – the first record is of a 'visit' to Cranmere Pool in 1789. But the railway, and Wordsworth's inspiration to the Victorian mind with a new view of 'the hills', combined to make Dartmoor the target for visitation, exploration and enjoyment that it remains. Hotels appeared in such villages as Chagford; other places – Yelverton, Moretonhampstead and Okehampton – sprouted short lines of villas in imitation of Malvern, Harrogate and Windermere. Before 1850 Chagford boasted guides for those 'desirous of investigating the moor'.

Inevitably interest in Dartmoor detail

South Brent railway station, on the main line between Exeter and Plymouth, is bustling with activity in this photograph from c. 1900

developed among the more leisured Devonian worthies – priests and businessmen to the fore. The broader minds like Burnard's recognized the wholeness of the 'grand old moor'. The Dartmoor Preservation Association sprang into life in 1883 to resist further enclosure of the Forest and the Commons, and soon it had to face a reservoir at Burrator and the beginnings of afforestation by the Duchy of Cornwall. Both Burnard and Hansford Worth, before the close of the nineteenth century, proposed that Dartmoor's future lay in some kind of park 'similar to ... the great American National Parks'.

Well, National Park it has become and, some hundred years after Worth's suggestion, the Dartmoor National Park Authority has been in business for about thirty-five years, though only for the last twelve has it had a full-time staff of consequence.

The Authority is a twenty-one-seat Committee of Devon County Council, but includes a member from each District Council and seven people appointed, to represent the 'national' interest in Dartmoor, by the Secretary of State. It is the local planning authority, while elsewhere that role is performed by the District Councils. It publishes, and reviews quinquennially, a National Park Plan, showing how it proposes to use its powers 'to preserve and enhance' the natural beauty and promote the enjoyment of Dartmoor, while having continuous regard for the social and economic well-being of its communities.

In pursuing these duties the Authority spends more than £1 000 000 in a year, three-quarters of it acquired directly from Whitehall. It uses that money on moorland and woodland management, car parks, lavatories and signposts. It maintains 500 miles of footpath and bridleway, clears tons of litter, repairs walls and riverbanks, and cares for and consolidates all kinds of historic and prehistoric structures. It makes grants for the maintenance of attractive traditional dwellings and compensates farmers who agree to particular restrictions or ways of farming. It works with other public agencies to improve the landscape and the services the remote communities need; in this it is assisted by large numbers of volunteers each year.

Its rangers keep a watchful eye on all kinds of recreation and their impact on land and locals; they keep the paths open, the signs up, the litter clear and the volunteers busy. Others plant trees, build buildings and advise upon, plan and control development. The Authority's staff liaise with every conceivable organization and individual, purist and philistine, whose ambitions might damage or enhance the face of Dartmoor. Yet others run information centres, guide walkers and produce the literature and the lectures that enlighten those who wish to know more.

It is they who have put together this book – a celebration of Dartmoor through the year, through the eyes of the National Park Authority. It may heighten perceptions of this compact but complex upland place and extend them from a summer Sunday to a winter Wednesday, from a sunlit flower head to a bleak, blurred skyline. With any luck it will illuminate, without pain or effort, the principles upon which the Dartmoor National Park Plan rests:

- the ecological truth of the interdependence of all life, including ours, and its dependence on earth, air and water;
- the role and skills of the farmer in managing landscapes;
- the gentle reconciliation of all forms of enjoyment with livelihoods and with each other;
- the growing art of the conservation of quality, not by stifling development or initiative, but combining the contentment of the local with the satisfaction of the visitor.

Do enjoy it.

IAN MERCER
Dartmoor National Park Officer

Spring

Postbridge

Vivid blue skies above the old clapper bridge and its neighbouring eighteenth century turnpike road bridge are reflected in the East Dart River. The clapper bridge was probably built during the thirteenth century alongside a ford crossing the river. With its massive slabs of rough granite, it was built to withstand fearful floods (sometimes the river rises to the very top of the piers, menacing the clapper stones!) and has done so fairly successfully through the centuries.

But in the mid 1970s it was noticed that one of the end piers was beginning to lean; the river was undermining it where the bank had been eroded by the force of the river in spate in the winter. The National Park Authority, with the County Engineers, raised the clapper stone with jacks and reformed the pier. An epoxy resin was used to make an invisible waterproof bond between the stones, and the river bank was restored with a facing of large boulders to prevent future damage. The old clapper bridge is ready for another few centuries of service!

The eastern moor

The sun picks out Bag Tor, small beside its neighbours, Haytor, Saddle Tor and Rippon Tor. The tor is on land enclosed by stone walls; such land is called a newtake and is not part of the commons. In the foreground is the wall of Bagtor Newtake with its little white hunt gate which was put in to allow access for the man whose job it was to put up the red flag when Rippon Tor rifle range (in use until 1977) was in action.

Beardown Man

There are a number of standing stones on Dartmoor, but most are connected with stone rows. Of the few isolated ones this is the most imposing; it is just west of Devil's Tor, and stands at 11 feet 4 inches. It was erected in prehistoric times and we can only guess at its significance.

Belted Galloway cattle

Up on the high north moor these cattle graze and thrive on heather and grass. Galloways are an old breed belonging to the type of black cattle that were forced, along with their Celtic owners, into the western fringes of the British Isles. These particular cattle, with a complete white band from shoulders to hips are now a distinct breed called Belted Galloway. Unlike Welsh Blacks, this breed is polled (without horns).

Galloways and the variant breeds are hardy and well suited to harsh climates and poor grazing. Their dense mossy undercoat enables them to stay out all winter where other breeds would not survive.

Primrose

A much-loved spring flower which needs no introduction; the sight and perfume of a mass of primroses in a Devon bank or the edge of a wood is a delightful experience. Primrose plants grow well in the right habitat but they do not propagate readily and grow very slowly. The plant lives for fifty or so years, so when one is destroyed, it is perhaps well to reflect that its life span would have been not so very much less than that of a human being.

Golden scale male fern

The new growth of this fern, arising phoenix-like from the old plant, seems to suggest the taut, ready-to-burst energy that is the essence of spring.

Ferns are amongst the world's most ancient surviving land plants; they are found as fossils over 300 million years old, and are still very primitive. They differ from other plants, for example, in that they do not have flowers; they reproduce by spores on the back of the leaf.

The damp climate of Dartmoor is ideal for ferns and many varieties are found. However, the royal fern – a particularly large handsome plant – has all but disappeared, as a result of the collection mania of fern enthusiasts in the nineteenth and twentieth centuries. Nowadays, since the 1981 Wildlife and Countryside Act, it is an offence to dig up and take any wild plants except certain weeds.

The East Okement valley

From this point on a very clear day you can see Exmoor. Even on a slightly cloudy day, as this was, the fields and woods in mid and north Devon make a view full of promise of interest. The walker is standing on the edge of Belstone Tor looking across the East Okement valley to Halstock Wood. Only a mile further down the valley the new Okehampton bypass runs.

Walla Brook on Cator Common

A beech tree leans over the clear reflecting water of a moorland stream, almost in the attitude of Narcissus as he admired his own image in warmer streams of Greek mythology.

Improved moorland

This view across the West Webburn valley to Hameldown is a good illustration of the impact of agricultural improvement on an upland landscape. The middle strip of Hameldown, called Blackaton Down, was fenced, ploughed and reseeded. The heather moorland has been entirely replaced by grassland, even right up to the skyline, which shows that much of Dartmoor, in spite of its height, poor soil and relatively cold wet climate, can be 'improved' agriculturally.

With the 'achievement' of surpluses in meat and cereals, the incentive to improve is disappearing from the hills in the late 1980s. Mechanisms such as management agreements can now be made by the National Park Authorities to prevent the wrong sort of change and compensate the farmer for any profit he foregoes in the process.

A Whiteface Dartmoor lamb

This sturdy little creature is about ten to fourteen days old and looks a credit to its mother. The breeding ewes on this particular farm on the west side of Dartmoor are brought into sheds in January. About three days after they have lambed the ewes and their lambs are turned out into the fields (unless there is snow in which case they stay in). Later on they go back up on to the common.

Dartmoors, like Devon Longwools and South Devons, are all large and heavy boned. The face is mainly white and well covered with wool which is generally long and curly. All these breeds are polled, although Dartmoor rams are occasionally horned.

Horse chestnut

The leaves of the horse chestnut are well advanced before the flowers (known as candles) come into bloom. By November in place of flowers are spiky green husks encasing large brown nuts, known to country children everywhere as conkers. Although the timber has little commercial value, this handsome tree is prized for the beauty of its blossom and its graceful height and shape.

Becky Falls

In winter and spring the Becka Brook makes a fine show thundering down the rocks, whilst in the summer, when thousands of visitors come to see the falls, the brook retreats almost entirely underneath the great boulders.
Crossing, who knew it in all seasons, described it thus:

> Here is a delightful picture of a tree-hidden dell, through which a little stream rushes down a steep and rocky channel, turning and twisting among rocky boulders, and forming numberless cascades. A charming retreat, where the heat of the summer day is exchanged for a delicious coolness. A spot always beautiful, whether it be when the sun has in part sealed up the springs of the stream, or whether it comes rushing down in a flood. *

*William Crossing, *Gems in a Granite Setting: beauties of the lone land of Dartmoor*, 1905, republished by Devon Books 1986.

A sheepdog at work

Here on Middle Merripit Farm at Postbridge one of the farm dogs singles out the required sheep at a word from the farmer. These border collies are willing workers, appearing to like nothing so much as being out on the hills working with sheep (these are Cheviot Cross) or cattle.

Pony trekking

The existence of pony-trekking stables on and around the moor enables many who would not otherwise have the chance the delight of experiencing the open space of Dartmoor on horseback.
The National Park Authority has a responsibility for trying to ensure that the effects of trekking on the peaty soil and vegetation are not unduly detrimental.

Rebuilding a bridge

Many of the rights of way on and around Dartmoor cross streams and rivers and are often furnished with small bridges. Here, over the Glaze Brook near South Brent, the decking of the bridge was rotten and the handrail unsafe. The National Park Authority undertook its repair as a routine matter of footpath maintenance. The first job was to strip off the rotten wood and creosote the two sturdy structural timbers. Then new decking was nailed on and the handrails replaced. The result is a strong safe bridge that should last for a further twenty or so years.

Okehampton Castle

Following his invasion in 1066, William the Conqueror imposed his rule on England. His harsh law made him extremely unpopular in the West Country and led to a great uprising in Exeter in 1068. In order to crush the rebellion, William appointed his nephew Baldwin as Sheriff of Devon and allowed him to choose a site to build a castle as his headquarters.

Baldwin chose a castle site on the banks of the West Okement and so marked the birth of the Norman town which developed at the river crossing nearby and which we now know as Okehampton. Though in a valley, the castle occupies a strong site on a spur of high ground made artificially higher, with a cleft on the west side above which towers a square keep. The keep may be late Norman in date but the other buildings mainly represent a rebuilding in about 1300. On the north side of the bailey are the remains of the great hall, kitchens, lodge, ward-rooms and a chapel. A mill, used for grinding the manor corn, once stood outside the main gates.

The ruins belong to the Department of the Environment and are open to the public during the summer.

Curlew's nest

Curlews nest in most damp moorland valleys on Dartmoor. They usually lay four eggs. Out of this clutch three have hatched, while the fourth is in the traumatic process of breaking out of the shell. In upland areas curlews do not start nesting until late May. During incubation, which lasts for four weeks, the parent birds take daily turns at sitting on the eggs, slipping quietly away from the nest if intruders come near.

Curlews, the largest of the waders, are resident all the year in Devon. They feed on coastal mud-flats during the winter but return to the moors or marshy meadows and fens to breed in the spring and summer. They are distinguished by their stately walk, the long curved beak with which they dig down to find the worms and grubs they live on, and, most of all, their evocative, melancholy, warbling call.

An early morning 'bird walk'

At 6.30 a.m. these enthusiastic early risers have joined a National Park guided walk. Birdsong is undoubtedly part of the natural beauty which National Parks exist to protect. It is at its best, and most easily heard and learnt, early in the morning before other noises intervene.

Willow warbler

This little bird, common all over the British Isles, builds its rather ragged nest on the ground. The nest is so well concealed that it is difficult to see that it has a domed roof. As a nesting area willow warblers favour scrub or damp places with alder and willow for they feed in the tree canopy. They breed in May and June and by the autumn the young birds are ready to undertake the remarkable 2500 mile journey to the land south of the Sahara Desert to pass the winter.

Devonport Leat above Whiteworks

The whiteness of dead purple moor grass lingers long into spring on the south moor. Above the Whiteworks buildings the Devonport Leat snakes around the hill. This leat was constructed in the 1790s to provide water for the burgeoning town of Devonport and still, nearly 200 years later, it indirectly supplies Plymouth, for part of its flow now feeds Burrator Reservoir. Down to the right are Foxtor Mires and behind Whiteworks is Royal Hill. Beyond is Bellever Forest and the long ridge on the skyline is Hameldown. Haytor and Rippon Tor are in the far right distance.

Whiteworks was one of the major nineteenth-century tin mines, although tin had been mined there in earlier years also. In the 1820s Whiteworks, Eylesbarrow and Vitifer were the only operating mines on Dartmoor. Whiteworks was worked off and on through most of the nineteenth century. Its name refers to the high quality 'white' tin that was found here.

Access to the moor at Holwell Lawn

A National Park ranger is constructing a stile to allow people to enter and walk over a moorland area which previously had no public access. The farmer had proposed to plough part of the land and notified the National Park Authority of his intention. In the end the two parties made an agreement for twenty-one years whereby the farmer, on receipt of a financial contribution, undertook to maintain the present character of the land and to allow the public freedom to walk on it.

In the first half of the 1980s the National Park made about thirty-five such management agreements. The land involved ranges in size from 4 acres to over 1300 acres. The agreements are usually concerned with preserving moorland vegetation. Many include the right of public access as part of the agreement and a few are designed to save specific ancient monuments or habitats from the plough.

Emsworthy

A similar agreement protects this landscape at the other end of the same farm.

Taw Marsh

Taw Marsh is an impressive bowl of a valley with the River Taw wandering tranquilly through it. Taw Head is just a mile north of Steeperton, the conical tor in the centre of the photograph, and the river flows north, turning east into Belstone Cleave to leave Dartmoor at Sticklepath, eventually reaching the north Devon Coast at Barnstaple. It is one of only three Dartmoor rivers (the others being its tributaries, the East and the West Okement) that run north.

The Water Authority extracts 2½ million gallons of water from Taw Marsh every day. The water is pumped from shallow wells which were sunk in the late 1950s and, because it was found to be radioactive, it is now passed through aeration tanks to release the radon gas. It then goes to Belstone treatment works and thence mainly to North Devon to supply houses, farms and businesses.

The Widecombe sign

In the winter of 1985–6, in response to a request from Widecombe Parish Council, the National Park Authority provided granite setts around this village sign to prevent further wear and tear on the ground from the thousands of visitors who each year examine it. It was designed by that well known parishioner Lady Sayer and erected in 1948 by Mr Hamlyn of Dunstone Manor.

Seen here setting the setts is the National Park Authority's foreman, helped by a girl on a Youth Training Scheme. About 1500 setts were used, which originally came from the Courage Brewery at Devonport.

Lydford Castle

Although this solid ruin is known as Lydford Castle, it was in fact the place where the tin miners held stannary courts and where they imprisoned in the damp basement those who offended against their laws. This gaol was dreaded by generation after generation of Dartmoor people for

First hang and draw
Then hear the cause, is Lydford Law.

The prison was built in 1195 and was used until the early 1600s. One famous case was that of the Member of Parliament for Plympton who was summoned in 1512 to the tinners' parliament on Crockern Tor because of his legislative efforts to prevent the tinners further silting up harbours with their excessive mining waste. For his trouble the tinners threw him into this 'heinous, contagious and detestable place'.

Today it is owned by English Heritage and freely open to the public.

Pearl bordered fritillary

Many butterflies begin to emerge in April or later and are a welcome reminder of the warm summer that each year we hope is imminent! The pearl bordered fritillary gets its name from the seven 'pearls' on the underside of its hind wing. The female lays her eggs on violets on which the caterpillars, when they emerge from the eggs, live. The caterpillar grows by shedding its skin or 'moulting'. After the fifth month it becomes a chrysalis and over-winters in this immobile form. By the spring of the following year a crumpled but fully formed butterfly emerges and the life cycle starts all over again.

There are between fifty and sixty varieties of butterfly in Britain. They are beautiful and entirely harmless insects, but sadly very much at risk from modern farming with its emphasis on herbicides and pesticides and the loss of wild land all over the country. The woodland fritillaries have suffered more particularly from a decline in traditional woodland management; the practice of coppicing provided glades or woodland clearings in which the food plants grew. However, in the South West some suitable habitats still exist and these butterflies are not uncommon.

Stocks at Belstone

A reminder of rough popular justice in previous centuries.

St Andrew's Church

One of the many lovely granite churches on the moor, the parish church at Moretonhampstead is also one of the most imposing. As in many parishes on Dartmoor, profits from the successful woollen and tin trades in the fifteenth and sixteenth centuries were given to enlarge, and sometimes rebuild, the existing small churches.

Walkers in the Erme valley

This lovely valley contains one of the three high-level relict woodlands of moorland Dartmoor – Piles Copse. It was protected from grazing animals, and so able to generate and grow, by the clitter fallen long ago from Sharp Tor above it. Some of the oaks are just visible in the valley bottom. On the other side of the valley a hardened track runs to the water-treatment works above Cornwood from a weir on the Erme. Under the track is a pipeline taking river water to these works.

Golden plover's nest

Since the 1950s small numbers (perhaps ten or so) of this lovely bird have been breeding on Dartmoor, which is the highest southernmost outpost of their normal breeding range. Golden plovers are so-called because of the golden colour lacing their dark topside plumage. It is a marvellous sight to see them wheeling in the air in a tightly formed flock or, as a group, feeding on the ground. They are easily identified by their habit of running and snatching at their prey (insects, fly larvae, worms, etc).

If the nest appears to be under threat, the parent birds will feign injury to draw attention away from the nest. It goes without saying that walkers, seeing this behaviour, should not distress the birds and put the nest at risk by staying in the area. Since 1981 (under the Countryside Act) it is a crime to kill or destroy any wild bird and, what is more, to kill or destroy its eggs.

Lichen and moss on granite

No Dartmoor granite boulder remains on the surface without eventually becoming covered with varieties of lichen (mainly the encrusting type) and moss too, if the aspect is not too dry. These are the first real colonizers of any bare ground.

Sheep shearing

The annual spring and early summer task of sheep shearing can be back breaking. Many farmers now enlist the help of contract shearers, as in this busy scene, for a good shearer can clear a fleece in two minutes or so, whereas it might take four or five minutes for those with less practice.

The wool is shorn not so much for the profit (less than £5 per fleece) but more for the welfare of the sheep themselves. Unshorn sheep tend to suffer from the heat and get 'flyblown' in long dirty wool.

A village blacksmith

The old trade of blacksmith has largely disappeared. Until the early part of this century every village of any size would have a smithy where the smith would shoe horses and make and mend all manner of agricultural and other tools. This particular blacksmith, who inherited the trade from his father, grandfather and great-grandfather, no longer shoes horses but turns his skill to items that are nowadays eminently saleable – fire grates and hoods, gates, railings, staircases and so on. The demand for such things means that the trade is finding a new lease of life.

Rethatching a roof

Thatched roofs, of which many remain on Dartmoor, need regular and expensive maintenance. The National Park Authority provides grant aid towards those costs because these traditional roofs are part of the texture of the rural scene. To match demand, there are now more thatchers in the Dartmoor area than there were in the 1960s and 1970s and most have full order books.

Thatch is made from either water reed or combed wheat reed. The wheat reed is a traditional by-product of the grain harvest. The corn is cut and put through the threshing machine which knocks the grain out but leaves the reed unbroken and aligned (combed) ready for thatching use. Wheat reed lasts about fifteen to twenty years if it has been organically grown. On Dartmoor this was almost always the standard roofing material.

Water reed is now also commonly used, although the ridge is always finished with the more flexible wheat reed. For the last twenty years or so the supply of water reed to Devon has mainly come from Austria. The Norfolk reed industry, although still operating, has suffered from excess application of agricultural fertilizers to the soil. The nitrates reduce the life of the reed, causing it to go black and break up after only a few years in the thatch. Good water reed will last about thirty-five years in the Dartmoor atmosphere and on the relatively low-pitched roofs.

Meldon Quarry

Just beyond the edge of the Dartmoor granite at Meldon, south-west of Okehampton, the rock is quarried extensively by British Rail. The stone, called hornfels (a sandstone metamorphosed by contact with the molten granite), is used to supply ballast for the Southern and Western Railway Regions. The quarry employs about sixty-two men; it covers 245 acres and annually produces 300 000 tons of rock. The railway line from Exeter is kept open as far as the quarry for the sole purpose of transporting the ballast.

Moor Brook

This stream rises just under West Mill Tor, which can be seen in the central distance, and runs on to join the East Okement River in Halstock Wood. Yes Tor, on the right, is part of the highest summit on Dartmoor. (High Willhays just behind it reaches 2039 feet.)

Early purple orchid

Early purple orchids produce bold bright spikes alongside many Dartmoor roads in late May and in June. This plant's preference for grassy banks means that it is still fairly common, unlike many of the fifty or so varieties of British orchids which grow in wet meadows and marshes. As those habitats have been dramatically reduced in recent decades some orchids are now rather rare.

Cuckoo flower

Otherwise known as lady's smock or milkmaid, this striking little whitey-mauve flower comes with spring, reputedly when the cuckoo first calls, and ends its flowering period at the same time that the cuckoo ceases to call. (It is strange that this should give the distinctive name, as many plants flower at just this period!) The long pointed leaves used to be picked and eaten in salads, which they improve with their slightly peppery flavour.

Harrowing

After ploughing, the soil needs to be further broken up. Drags or (as here) disc harrows are used.

Pigs at leisure

At one time it was normal for every cottager to have a pig in a sty near his cottage. Some Dartmoor farmers still like to keep a pig or two for they are economical to rear and, being intelligent creatures, are entertaining to watch.

Fox

In the early morning light this fox quickly noses its way along the top of a hedge looking for what provides part of its normal staple diet – worms, slugs, beetles, frogs, mice and birds eggs. You can see the well-known 'red' colour of its coat, with the white throat and underbelly.

During the winter the dog fox seeks out a vixen. After mating, which may involve several male foxes fighting over a female, and a lot of barking and screaming, the pair will find and make a den, often in an old hole such as a badger sett. In April from three to six cubs are born. The mother teaches them to hunt and within two months they are ready to leave. The vixen and dog also leave the den and part company once the breeding season is over.

An ancient tenement

Here the West Dart runs alongside fields belonging to Dunnabridge which is one of the thirty-five original 'ancient tenements' in the Dart valley. The ancient tenements were freehold farms which lay wholly within the Forest of Dartmoor (so-called because it was the medieval royal hunting ground), occupying land north and west of Dartmeet. Although their existence is first documented in the mid thirteenth century, these settlements may be much older in origin: the surrounding field patterns (small square fields) are more characteristic of the Celtic (pre-Saxon) period than of late medieval times.

Nun's Cross

Otherwise known as Siward's Cross, this is one of the largest, and perhaps the finest, of the crosses on Dartmoor which mark routes across its sometimes featureless wastes. It is also the earliest of which we have written evidence; it was mentioned in the perambulation of 1240, although certainly many other crosses existed by that date.

In the background is Nun's Cross Farm. This little farm was one of the last to be enclosed from the common in the period between 1750 and 1880. It was a farming labourer called John Hooper who took this initiative, and in 1871, one year after he built the farmhouse, he was visited by William Crossing, the famous Dartmoor walker. Crossing recorded that after putting up the farmhouse and buying a cow, John Hooper had no more than 4d. left 'to go on with'. However, through hard work he prospered and by the end of his life was selling £100 worth of head of cattle yearly.

The farm was worked until some time after the Second World War, when it fell into disuse. It is now used by a school as a base for outdoor activities.

Cottages in Lustleigh

Lustleigh is a small village (parish population some 600 souls) with cottages compactly clustered about the fine granite church. Around are steep wooded hills in which are the houses built by the Victorians and Edwardians who thought it an idyllic place to settle once the Newton Abbot–Moretonhampstead railway of 1866 made it accessible.

'Battle' near Burrator

In the spring of 1985 the Burrator area was transformed by an invasion of tented encampments, soldiers, horses, waggons, guns, corpses – all the horror of a full-scale (if old-fashioned) war, one would think, until the camera-crew van is spotted beyond the nearest stone wall. The filming of part of *Revolution*, a Goldcrest production, took place here. It is claimed that parts of Dartmoor are nearer in appearance to the eighteenth-century up-state New York landscape than the state itself now. Dartmoor is in fact a fairly popular place for filming anything from scenes in feature films to television advertisements.

Norsworthy Bridge near Burrator Reservoir

By late spring the leaves on the oak trees have lost their early reddish tinge and become fully green. The wild yellow flags are in bloom and a heavy dew still lies on the grass before the morning sun dispels it.

Steps Bridge

The wild daffodils of the Teign valley are well-known and loved by the people of Dunsford and other nearby villages and even as far afield as Exeter and Torquay. Indeed, until the mid 1960s buses would come from Exeter and their passengers would go home laden with daffodils in bags, buckets and washing baskets! It became apparent that the daffodils were decreasing in number. In 1966 the Devon Trust for Nature Conservation acquired part of the valley and, with the help of volunteers, persuaded people that to look and enjoy was pleasure enough. Since then the habit of picking the flowers has gradually died and every April we can see

> . . . daffodils
> That come before the swallow dares, and take
> The winds of March with beauty
>
> (Shakespeare, *The Winter's Tale*)

An old tractor

This David Brown 950 is about thirty years old and sports one large truck wheel at the front, which must make interesting driving. Dartmoor is truly a graveyard of venerable agricultural implements. This tractor's most recent job was hedge trimming, now nearly always done by the ubiquitous flail. Farmers tend to get round to this job in late August and September when silage, hay and harvest are all safely in. They (or any landowner with roadside hedges) are responsible for cutting back the annual growth; highway authorities cut only 'visibility splays' or level verges 3 feet from the tarmac.

Blackthorn blossom

The tiny starry white flowers open in March on the spiney black branches of the blackthorn, well before its leaves are out. By autumn the flowers that are pollinated have become round blue-black sloes.

The blackthorn is a robust tree, never growing more than 12 or so feet high, and able to withstand the icy moorland wind and hungry animals where few other trees survive that double onslaught.

Woods and fields

From Fatherford railway viaduct this view to the south shows the East Okement valley. Halstock Wood on the right is a Site of Special Scientific Interest. Since this photograph was taken in 1986 a second viaduct carrying the Okehampton bypass has been constructed in the foreground of this scene.

Ponies at Sourton Tors

Dusk falls while unconcerned ponies graze quietly beside one of the Sourton Tors.

This century, with the introduction of Scotch Blackface sheep and Galloway cattle, the ponies have had to compete with them for food in the winter (see page 116). In earlier times only the ponies were left on the moor.

Ponies also have to compete with the fact that cattle and sheep are valuable in terms of government subsidies (paid per head). Ponies produce many more offspring over the years, but they carry no subsidy. Fifty years ago there were 25 000 ponies on the moor; in 1986 pony keepers registered only 2500 as grazing. How many will be left at the end of the century?

Summer

The River Dart at Spitchwick

On this mild summer day the River Dart is seen passing through perhaps its best-loved area – Deeper Marsh on Spitchwick Common. At first glance it is a natural enough scene, but a closer look at the river bank will reveal the hand of man, or, to be more accurate, the effect of a powerful earthmoving machine operated most delicately by the National Park Authority works foreman.

By the late seventies the river bank had become very badly eroded and this lovely area was beginning to look a mess. The erosion occurred from too many people using the river bank as they would the seaside – for example, taking buckets and spades and digging into the turf. Once the turf had gone, the winter floods scoured away the sandy soil underneath.

The irregular 'boulder' which now forms the river bank allows people access to the water to paddle, but prevents erosion. New soil was placed behind the boulders and seeded to form a pleasant picnic area.

Marsh marigold

The brilliant golden flowers of marsh marigold sometimes brighten wet wooded valleys around the fringes of the moor. It is also called kingcup.

Bluebells on Pepperdon Down

The bluebell is a native flower which is normally found in shady woods but will also grow on open heath, making its characteristic carpet of blue. It flowers in early June and the scent is sweet and delicate.

Scotch Blackface sheep with lamb

Because of their hardiness, the Scotch Blackface sheep are the most common breed found on the upland commons of Dartmoor. The rams are put with the flock in November (tupping, as it is called), so that the ewes do not lamb until March or April after a five-month gestation period. From sheep grazing out on the hills one lamb from each ewe is as much as the farmer can expect, indeed if they gave birth to twins they could hardly feed both. A hill ewe in lamb may lose up to one third of her weight between autumn and spring, and a barren ewe even more. So summer is the time for the ewes and ewe lambs to eat well, preparing for the rigours of the forthcoming winter and spring

In autumn the lamb sales are held and the ram lambs are sold on to lowland farmers to fatten. Their meat is lean and so currently much in favour with butchers. The best ewe lambs are kept for breeding and will be put to the ram in the following November so that they start their breeding period when they are eighteen months old (at this stage they are called 'two tooth', a name based on their dental development).

An inquisitive calf

A calf explores the woodland at the edge of its field.

Grimspound

This is among the most accessible and impressive of surviving prehistoric villages. It consists of a stout perimeter wall, which is reckoned to have originally been at least 6 feet high and 9 feet wide, enclosing some twenty-four huts.

The people who lived here from about 2000 B.C. knew the arts of pottery making, flint working, animal husbandry, the cultivation of grain and how to smelt tin and copper to make bronze. Grimspound was only one of many settlements where generations of these peaceful pastoralists lived for perhaps several centuries. It must have been inconceivable in that warmer drier Dartmoor clime that the world would ever change!

Hay turning

After the grass has been cut it is left to dry in the field for a few days. During this period it must be turned at least once, and more if it rains. This is an essential part of drying the hay and a very thick or young crop will require more attention. At this stage in his year's work, above all others, the farmer prays for fine weather.

Lynchets at Challacombe

The ridges to the left of the dry stone wall on the far slope are known as 'lynchets' and are the remains of medieval strip fields. On a sloping hillside such as this the soil that was thrown downhill by the plough for year upon year formed little terraces which then defined the boundaries of the cultivation strips.

In the Middle Ages the land was worked by a number of tenant farmers from the nearby hamlet of Challacombe, which is now no more than a single farm. Each farmer cultivated several separate strips in the area.

This was a common feudal arrangement in all parts of England. However, strips such as these are almost unique on Dartmoor, where fields more usually developed as small rectangular or squarish plots, individually owned and used. The lynchets in this valley are now the subject of a management agreement whereby the owner undertakes not to destroy them and to control growth of bracken on them in return for an annual compensation from English Heritage.

Beech woods

The sun has coaxed the beech buds into leaf and here makes a pattern recalling Gerard Manley Hopkins' famous line: 'Glory be to God for dappled things . . .'

A badger emerging from its sett

The inoffensive badger has no natural enemies other than man who over centuries has made a pastime of badger digging and baiting. Today these 'sports' are illegal but on Dartmoor the unfortunate badger still suffers from the attention of man, for it is now associated with tuberculosis in cattle and thought to be a carrier of this disease. The evidence for this connection is disputed but MAFF (the Ministry of Agriculture, Fisheries and Food) has for some years been attempting to cull members of the badger population in areas where T.B. outbreaks occur in cattle.

Badgers are not often seen for they are nocturnal animals; nevertheless they are widespread and numerous on Dartmoor. They usually live in family or social groups in an underground sett which consists of chambers and tunnels about 10–20 yards long and with several entrances. The sett is kept clean; fresh bedding of dried leaves, grass and bracken is taken in on dry nights and the badgers dig shallow holes away from the sett for use as latrines. They live on small mammals, slugs, snails, earthworms, berries and even grass.

Buttercup

This species is common all over England and Wales but particularly fond of damp meadows such as are found on farms on the fringes of Dartmoor. It gets its name from the belief that if it was rubbed on a cow's udder the milk would improve in quality. It flowers all through the summer, though it is most prolific in June, and is carefully avoided by grazing cattle and sheep, for it is poisonous. When the poet Robert Browning was in Italy and homesick for England he thought of the humble buttercup.

Foxglove

Triumphantly tall, the foxglove stands out above all the other summer flowers in the Devon hedgerow. Here forget-me-not and campion form a colourful background. Each stem of the foxglove can bear anything from twenty to eighty flowers; as those lower down die new ones open higher up the stem. All parts of the plant are poisonous; it contains the powerful drug digitalin which slows down the rate of the heart beat and in controlled quantities is still used in the treatment of heart disease.

Cutting back bracken

These children from London were staying for a week at the Dartmoor Training Centre at Prince Hall. As part of their week they spent a day working with a National Park Ranger, an arrangement which is commonly made by schools using the Centre. They are shown here at Coombe Farm, Cornwood, cutting back bracken which was steadily encroaching into a meadow rich in wild flowers and insects.

Cows near Hennock

At five o'clock on a June morning a golden light illuminates the land. The cows make the most of the hour or two before they are called in for milking. Walt Whitman's line is apt: 'I think I could turn and live with animals, they're so placid and self contained'.

Down Tor stone row

This is one of the most impressive of the sixty or more stone rows that still exist from prehistoric days on Dartmoor. At one end it adjoins a stone circle which was the retaining wall of a barrow or burial mound, now no longer very obvious. The end stone, which has been re-erected, stands 9½ feet high and the row is 382 yards in length.

Spinsters' Rock

There are only a few chambered tombs on Dartmoor and Spinsters' Rock is certainly the most impressive. In 1862 the uprights fell down but were restored in the same year, though not, unfortunately, to their exact original position. These multiple burial tombs are the earliest graves known on the moor, possibly dating back to about 3500 B.C.

The tomb's name comes from the legend of the three spinsters (or spinners) who were said to have erected it one morning before breakfast! It stands in a private field; to allow public access, in 1985 the National Park Authority negotiated a management agreement with the owner.

Beating the bounds

Most parishes undertake to 'beat their bounds' every now and then although often twenty or more years may elapse between each beating. In medieval times this custom was a way of ensuring that the parish boundary remained the same from one generation to the next. The children were 'bumped' on the boundary stones or other markers to make them remember the line of the boundary. Most parish boundaries are too long to walk in one day and must be split into two or three days' walking. Often they follow streams or may traverse woods or moor where the going is rough. Here a party from Hennock parish walk a stretch of road which marks part of the boundary.

Wild plants in a gateway

By late July the hedgerow growth is at its peak with the grass now long and heavy with seed. Many other plants have seeded, here in particular dock (reddish) and lamb's tongue. Still flowering are vetch, yarrow, woundwort and, most dominant, cow parsley.

Cadover Bridge

Many visitors to the moor enjoy the easy access to a river (here the Plym) where a road crosses it. At Cadover Bridge and for half a mile upstream on a Sunday anything up to 5000 people, mainly families, relax and enjoy the moor air, the shallow clear waters and the turf, heather and rocks of the surrounding terrain.

Field walls at Babeny

The farmer of this ancient tenement in the East Dart valley decided some years ago that the walls of his small fields were no longer practical under modern farming methods. It was difficult to make silage (the machinery being unmanoeuvrable in the small fields) and a number of walls were in a ruinous state and so not stockproof. He informed the National Park Authority, who realized the potential damage to the landscape, of his intention to level many of the walls.

The outcome was one of the earliest 'management agreements' on Dartmoor whereby the farmer agreed to keep the most ancient walls and only level more recent ones, and the National Park Authority estate team rebuilt the remaining walls to make them stockproof. No money changed hands and the main elements of an historic landscape still exist.

River Walkham

A typical moorland river flows between the rocks with its clear waters, the bracken and willow on its banks, and a tor (Great Mis Tor) looming above it. This river valley in late medieval times must have been alive with activity. As in most Dartmoor valleys alluvial tin was present. It had probably been extracted since early medieval times or before and smelted by primitive means. However, in the early fourteenth century the smelting process was greatly improved by progression to the more efficient and sophisticated blowing houses.

Remains of a blowing house

Today there are still the remains of several of these blowing houses in the Walkham valley. These generally date to before 1750, from a time when both crushing and smelting took place in the same building. In many of the ruins are old granite mortar stones, hollowed out by the action of water-powered stamps crushing the ore. When the ore had been smelted, the molten tin was poured into mouldstones, as in this picture, to make ingots.

Hexworthy Tin Mine

This mine was opened, or rather reopened as it was the site of much older workings, in 1890. It was highly productive until about 1909 and in those years employed about fifty men and produced a total of 191 tons of black tin. Thereafter work continued, although with a lower turnover, into the 1920s.

This photograph shows the old dressing floor where the ore was crushed and separated again and again so that the sandy waste could be discarded and the tin ore became more concentrated. There were various ways of doing this at different stages, including shaking tables and (the circular remains in the photograph) revolving buddles. These latter depended upon centrifugal force, which, as they turned, edged the worthless sand, which was lighter, to the edge, while the heavier tin ore stayed in the middle. To begin with the buddles and other machinery were powered by water, and the old wheel pit has recently been restored by the National Park Authority. Later on the machinery was electrically turned, the electricity being generated by a Pelton wheel over a mile down the O Brook valley, which the company installed in 1905.

The site was used during the Second World War as target practice; many of the shell holes are still obvious in the remaining walls.

Sundew

This remarkable little bog plant manages to supplement its required nutrients (inadequate from the poor acid bog in which it grows) by catching and digesting small insects. The leaves are covered with sticky red hairs which trap the insects when they land. The leaves then curl around, digesting and absorbing the insect.

This is a typical picture of the plant; the flower heads are normally seen in bud form, opening only in very specific conditions. However, the plant does propagate by seed as well as vegetatively.

Cotton grass

The sight of white bobbing cotton grass heads usually means wet ground, for this plant thrives everywhere on Dartmoor where the soil is poorly drained and boggy. Each of the fine white hairs is attached to a seed, enabling dispersal by the wind.

Local patron outside village pub

The Drewe Arms in Drewsteignton is one of only two remaining pubs on Dartmoor which have a tap room rather than a bar. It is also remarkable in its landlady; Mrs Mudge, ninety-one years of age in 1986, must surely be the oldest licensee in Great Britain. In good health now, she sees no reason to retire. She and her husband took over the pub from other members of the family in 1919, and when in 1951 Mr Mudge died, Aunt Mabel, as she is known, took over the licence.

It is a convivial place for a drink. In the small room with wooden benches around the wall one finds an open friendly atmosphere, general conversation, and, now and then, delightful music and song.

School children on a field trip

Many schools use Dartmoor as an educational resource where the teachers can enliven some of the topics learned in the classroom. Here the children are learning ways of measuring the flow of a river, in this case the Cherry Brook. Through the mediation of the National Park Education Officer, they have obtained the necessary permissions of landowner and tenant.

Bog asphodel

The yellow head of the bog asphodel is a shaft of bright colour in the wet land where it thrives. Its Latin name, Narthecrium ossifragum (or breakbones), refers, it is claimed, to one of two things: either the lack of calcium in the moorland soil and consequently fragile bones in the moorland stock, or the danger of breaking legs when a pony stumbles into the bog.

Marsh St John's wort

With its leaves decked with dew drops and reminiscent in shape of an eastern pagoda, this modest plant is common in the acid valley bogs of Dartmoor. Between June and September the downy tower is topped by a small bright-yellow flower.

Fishing at Spitchwick

Migratory fish ascend Dartmoor's rivers from spring onwards, but autumn is the time for the main run.

The tree-lined pools of the River Dart at Spitchwick provide opportunities for salmon to rest on their journey from the sea to the spawning beds high up on the moor. Here the angler, searching the river with an artificial fly of fur and feather, can hope. Quite why the salmon, which do not feed in fresh water, should take a gaudy concoction of feather and fur is something of a mystery, but luckily for the angler they do.

The open season for fishing (both salmon and trout) varies from river to river but generally speaking runs from spring to autumn.

Widecombe-in-the-Moor

The village of Widecombe is tiny; most of the population of the parish live in the scattered farms, houses and hamlets surrounding the village in the peaceful East and West Webburn valleys.

The more sheltered valleys and 'in-country' on and around the moor inevitably attract a considerable pressure for new dwellings, usually bungalows. The desire to build and live in beautiful countryside is understandable. Unfortunately 'those who have the view also spoil it' (as was said of the plotlanders in the 1930s who set up shanties in idyllic rural scenes in the south-east of England).

Since 1947 planning policies have dictated a presumption against unnecessary new building in the countryside. The government has decreed that there be the most strict adherence to these policies within the National Parks since these areas have more to lose by a widespread proliferation of new buildings. The Dartmoor National Park planners probably do more than anyone to keep Dartmoor free from unsightly development of all kinds whilst trying to cater for the local essential needs.

The task is not easy and local popularity is not always a feature of this job; everyone likes to be able to do what they want with their own land. However, one only needs to travel to one of the many countries where planning control is weak or non-existent to see how whole areas of beautiful countryside and coast are being engulfed by tarmac and concrete. In looking at this peaceful rural landscape we should recall that good planning practice has on the whole kept it from the same fate.

Litter

Summer brings many crops, the least desirable being the annual crop of litter left behind after the car-borne trippers have departed. One of the worst-hit areas is Roborough Down, only 8 miles from the centre of Plymouth with its quarter of a million inhabitants. Most litter is merely dirty and unsightly, but occasionally it presents a bizarre appearance, as with this doll's head on Roborough Down. The Rangers pick up, with much volunteer help, 6000 bags of loose litter annually.

Deliberate dumping (here at Tolchmoor Gate) also produces rubbish that the Area Ranger has to clean up; it amounts to about 200–250 trailer loads a year. However, in this case prosecutions are sometimes successfully brought against the culprits.

New shoes all round

The pony stands placidly as steam and smoke issue from its hoof where the farrier presses the red-hot shoe against it. Most farriers (or blacksmiths) now travel to their customers. They are able to carry a small portable (electric, gas or hand-operated) forge and all other tools in a van. They also carry with them ready-made shoes rather than making them individually, as used to be done, for each horse. This is a good instance of new technology changing the practice of a trade.

Apple crusher at Longstone

Longstone was one of the farms that had to be abandoned in the late 1890s to give way to the waters of the newly built Burrator Reservoir. Here, with grass and weeds encroaching on it, is the farm apple crusher. The upper wheel, drawn by a horse, rolled around the edge of the trough reducing the apples to pulp (which was thrown to the pigs) and juice which, when fermented, became cider.

Modern agriculture

New techniques of farming come to Dartmoor eventually and this – the big baler – is one which saves the farmer much work and worry. It can make silage as well as hay, although of the two silage is more popular because it does not have to wait under the fickle English sun to dry, it is more nutritious for the cattle and it can be cut earlier so that two cuts can be taken before the end of the season.

Here, at Hurston Farm, Chagford, silage is being made. The grass has lain for two days to wilt slightly and is then baled up. The cylindrical bales are lifted by an hydraulic spike on the back of the tractor, or on its fore-end loader, and taken to the bale heap usually in a convenient corner of the field. There a black plastic bag is pulled over the bale while it is still airborne and the bag is carefully tied so as to exclude all air. The grass slowly ferments within the bags and when winter comes it is ready for the farmer to carry on the tractor spike straight to the cattle. Each bale weighs about half a ton and will provide keep for twenty to twenty-five cattle for one day.

Sheep dipping

Regular dipping protects sheep against various diseases – flystrike, lice and particularly sheep scab which is a parasitic mite living on the skin. In 1952, after a major national effort, scab was eradicated in Great Britain but unfortunately it reoccurred in 1973. The effect on the sheep of this highly contagious scourge can be devastating – irritation, distress, loss of condition and fleece, and finally death. The Ministry of Agriculture, Fisheries and Food is therefore still trying to eliminate this notifiable disease by insisting on regular dipping twice a year (summer and autumn). Officials from the Trading Standards Department are present to check that the dip is of the correct strength and the sheep properly immersed for the required length of time. The wild moor sheep fight desperately against being pushed under the evil-smelling dip and emerge snorting, panting and dripping.

The River Teign above Fingle Bridge

As with most of the other Dartmoor rivers, the Teign has carved a deep gorge for itself where it crosses the 'metamorphic aureole' – the rock around the edge of the granite. The walk from Steps Bridge up to Dogmarsh Bridge (about 6½ miles) follows the river through the Fingle Gorge past such lovely scenes as these.

On either side it is heavily wooded. A walker writing in 1864 says, 'Nature here is most lavish of her gifts, the Oak, Ash, Alder, Silver Birch, and Mountain Ash or Rowan, thickly interspersed with Hazel bushes, clothe the hillsides and fringe the streams with their rich green foliage ....'* Until the 1920s and 1930s charcoal burning was a regular industry in these woods, which on upper slopes were mainly oak. The last gasp of the industry was during the Second World War when home-grown charcoal was needed once more.

Today the industry here is conifer plantation. Trees have been planted in blocks along the Teign valley and now occupy about 60 per cent of the valley. However, under a 1985 Amendment to the Forestry Act the remainder of the oak woods are now safe, both here in the Teign valley and anywhere else in the country where it might have been a commercial proposition to replace broadleaf trees with conifers.

**A Gentleman's Walking Tour of Dartmoor* (Devon Books, 1986)

Damselfly

This delicate and vivid insect is very similar to a dragonfly but slightly smaller and even more slender. Both live near water, feeding on mosquitos and other small flies. The head consists mainly of two huge compound eyes for all-round and extremely sensitive vision. The life of a damselfly is over in one year. The nymphs emerge in summer from eggs laid in a slow-moving stream or still water. The nymph grows steadily, feeding on smaller insects and shedding its skin several times. In the following year, tempted by the warmth of the late spring sun, it crawls up the stem of a water plant and sheds its final skin to reveal the beautiful creature seen here. But beauty fades fast; in a few short weeks the damselfly has laid eggs and died.

Greater woodrush

Woodrushes differ from true rushes which have narrow, smooth, rigid leaves whilst the woodrush has flat pliable leaves with long white hairs on their edges. Woodrushes (and rushes in general) are flowering plants although the flowers are not conspicuous, being small and brown in colour. Greater woodrush is a common woodland plant and carpets the damp floor in, for example, the woods of the Teign valley.

Limekiln at Meldon

This late-eighteenth-century limekiln, one of the oldest existing on Dartmoor, is tucked into the side of the West Okement valley, downstream from the stained concrete face of Meldon Dam and below the elegant Victorian structure of Meldon Viaduct. The interior of the kiln was becoming increasingly ruinous and in 1984 the National Park estate team undertook the very tricky job of restoring it, partly for its rarity and partly for safety as this area is used more by the public since the construction of Meldon Reservoir.

Abandoned corbels at Swell Tor Quarry

Quarrying for stone on Dartmoor was mainly a nineteenth-century phenomenon when it became a massive industry. One of the two large quarrying areas was west of Princetown where four major quarries were operating, though not continuously, from 1820 until the First World War. One of these, Merrivale, is still working.

These elaborately worked stones, 9 feet long, which lie on a siding leading into the old Swell Tor Quarry, were cut in 1903 as corbels for London Bridge. They were awaiting collection by the little railway that once served the quarries and Princetown; it was horse-drawn from 1823 until nearly the end of the nineteenth century. Surplus to requirements they lie here still, a fine testimonial to the skill of the masons who worked in these quarries.

The Dartmoor Folk Festival

Since the mid 1970s this event has become a fixture in the Dartmoor calendar. It is held on the second weekend in August at the village of South Zeal. Musicians, dancers and folk enthusiasts come from many parts of the West Country to take part in concerts, competitions, pub singing, dances and the general musical and friendly ambience.

Water crowfoot

Found in streams and ponds, water crowfoot lives at the surface of the water with its roots and finer leaves submerged while the flat leaves and flowers float.

Water forget-me-not

This delicate flower is a native perennial found on Dartmoor in the boggy areas beside moorland streams or in the shallows of rivers after they have left the moor. It is one of eight varieties of forget-me-not found in Britain.

A wary rabbit listens and watches

Rabbits, perhaps surprisingly, are not native to this country; they were introduced by the Normans in the eleventh century. Until the beginning of the nineteenth century they were scarce as various creatures preyed upon them, including peasants in the grip of winter hunger. It was even worth setting up warrens on Dartmoor from early Norman times to 'farm' rabbits for their meat.

However, at the end of the eighteenth century, gamekeepers began a massive slaughter of predatory birds and animals. At the same time, in the new Agricultural Revolution, crops such as turnips and kale were grown for winter feeding of farm animals, incidentally providing rabbits with winter food. This interference with nature led to an imbalance; rabbits multiplied fantastically and became a major pest, despite the huge numbers killed by man for food and fur. It was estimated that by 1950 there could be as many as 100 million rabbits in the country.

Then in 1954 the dreadful disease of myxomatosis wiped out about 99 per cent of the rabbit population. Very gradually rabbits have returned to Devon, but only in limited numbers, for myxomatosis is endemic and, although not as effective as in its first strike, it still wipes out local groups of rabbits.

Leather Tor above Burrator Reservoir

The two consecutive dry summers of 1976 and 1977 led to severe drought in the West Country. This usually brimming reservoir dropped lower and lower, exposing rocks never normally seen.

Common blue on green alkanet

This is one of the most widespread of butterflies, often seen on the open grassy spaces of Dartmoor. Its main larval food plant is clover.

Tavistock Abbey

These low grey ruins in the centre of Tavistock are all that remains of the largest and wealthiest of Benedictine Abbeys. It was founded in the tenth century and flourished for nearly 600 years until, like all other similar monastic houses, it was dissolved by Henry VIII. The ruins are of Hurdwick stone from quarries north of Tavistock. When the seventh Duke of Bedford totally replanned and rebuilt the centre of Tavistock in the mid nineteenth century the same handsome greenish stone was used. Tavistock was one of three medieval monasteries whose wealth and influence extended far over Dartmoor. Buckland and Buckfast were the others.

Stepping stones over the East Dart

The monkey-flower, originally introduced from North America, but now successfully established along some British rivers and streams, decorates these mossy stepping stones near Prince Hall.

A frog partly camouflaged by its surroundings

The frog is an animal that features in many food chains, eaten by nearly every predator. As tadpoles they are eaten by fish, newts, water insects and water birds so that only a small proportion of the 2000 to 3000 eggs laid by the mother survive to become adult frogs. But then as adults they are hunted and eaten by snakes, rats, hedgehogs, foxes, pike, otters, herons and others. Frogs in turn eat worms, insects, slugs and snails.

Adders

Adders are relatively common on Dartmoor and everyone is familiar with their zig-zag back pattern, for they are Britain's only poisonous snake. In fact they are not very poisonous; normal reaction to a bite is pain, swelling and discolouration in the immediate area, usually followed by vomiting – unpleasant indeed, but hardly ever fatal.

During the winter snakes hibernate under rocks or in crevices. They emerge in spring and mating takes place in May. The young (usually between five and twenty) are born live in September (in this they differ from most snakes who start life in an egg) and are immediately independent. The feed chiefly on small mammals, such as mice or voles, and a large meal may last them for a week.

Adders, like most snakes, are much misunderstood and wrongly feared and loathed. They are normally inoffensive, timid creatures; knowing instinctively that only one light footstep on their soft unprotected back means death to them, they slip away as fast as they can if they hear the clumsy tread of a large animal or person approaching.

Harvesting

Until the late 1950s corn cut in the field and left to dry in stooks of six sheaves was a common sight. The stooks usually stood for a period of 'three bells' (or Sundays) to dry. Then the combine harvester which cuts and threshes in one operation made the old process redundant. However, this machine, though remarkably efficient, is not suitable if good wheat straw is required for thatching. A few farms around Dartmoor harvest in the old way to supply the demand for long unbroken thatching straw. On this particular farm in the Teign valley wheat sheaves are gathered in every year and threshed on a threshing machine which is more than 100 years old.

Powder Mills

This lovely area is enhanced by the remains of a gunpowder factory built on the banks of the Cherry Brook in the mid nineteenth century. Known as the Powder Mills, the factory did well until the 1890s when it closed, the use of gunpowder for mine and quarry blasting having been overtaken by the invention of dynamite. These buildings are in private enclosed land but can be seen from the main road between Postbridge and Two Bridges and from a public right of way that passes nearby.

Tavy Cleave

The Tavy and its tributaries drain the wild wet peat-bound area of Rattlebrook, Kneeset, Fur Tor and Cut Hill. The river then runs south-west through the steep and rocky Tavy Cleave, leaving the moor to pass through Tavistock and join the Tamar just north of Plymouth. Most of the time the only sound in the Cleave is the stream's placid murmur, but after heavy rain this can be transformed into a frightening roar, amplified by the granite battlements towering above it.

Bell heather and western gorse

The striking contrast between these two vividly coloured flowers which are frequently found together is one of the summer joys of Dartmoor. Both are often mistaken for other similar plants. Bell heather can be distinguished from cross-leaved heath as the latter has slightly larger, pale pink flowers, and western gorse differs from common gorse, mainly because it is smaller, but also the prickles or spines of the western gorse are curved.

Cottages in Buckfastleigh

Buckfastleigh is one of the distinctive small towns around the edge of Dartmoor. In the nineteenth century the town became an industrial centre where the waters of the River Mardle were used to power no less than five woollen mills as well as others milling corn and paper. The population nearly doubled between 1801 and 1901 and cottages like these were built to house the mill workers. This industry only recently failed; the last woollen mill in Buckfastleigh closed in 1975 although at nearby Buckfast the woollen mill is a thriving concern producing yarn from Scotch Blackface sheep on Dartmoor for Axminster carpets.

Most of the mill buildings have been demolished; those that remain are now used for a variety of light industries. The tannery still survives as a fellmongery (where sheep skins are processed into rugs) and nearby at the Wool Board premises fleeces from all over the South West are collected and graded. But the collapse of the woollen industry left in its wake much unemployment which tourism could only partly fill and the townspeople have had to commute to find work.

Pony and foal

While mother grazes, the young colt apprehensively watches the quiet approach of the photographer.

This mare probably started breeding when she was two to three years old, mating with the stallion which defends her herd. She comes into season again nine days after the birth of her foal which will suckle right up until the time she gives birth again, eleven months later. If she survives all the obstacles of life on Dartmoor and stays reasonably fit she may continue with this cycle for seventeen or more years.

Barnyard cock

This barnyard cock stands framed in a splendid granite doorway at Corndon Ford which was a new feature added to the old farmhouse in 1718. The seventeenth and eighteenth centuries were a period of prosperity for the farmers of Dartmoor, based on a long steady boom in the woollen trade. Many of the Dartmoor farmhouses had porches and other improvements made to them in this period.

> While the cock with lively din,
> Scatters the rear of darkness thin,
> And to the stack, or the barn door,
> Stoutly struts his dames before.
>
> (Milton, *L'Allegro*)

Sam's scrapyard

This well-hidden corner of Dartmoor is the last resting home of defunct cars and vehicles of all kinds, stoves, fridges and farm machinery, before they are ultimately squashed into bales of scrap metal. Under the benevolent and generous management of its founder-owner and occupier, Mr Sam Harris, local farmers benefit, not only by the ready availability of spare parts, but by the clean-up collections of derelict cars and machines from their farmyards and fields. All transactions here are a pleasure, seasoned with remarkable anecdotes and rare good humour.

Coach crossing New Bridge

Owned by a local firm which specializes in day tours on Dartmoor, this coach is a 'narrow-bodied' forty-five seater, specially designed to go over the three difficult narrow bridges in the Dart valley – Holne Bridge, New Bridge and (even narrower!) Huccaby Bridge. The road from Ashburton to Dartmeet is in fact closed to both caravans and vehicles over 33 feet long and wider than 8 feet 5 inches (New Bridge is only 8 feet 6 inches). Vehicles that ignore the many signs are disobeying the law and cause lengthy jams and furious frustration for other road users and often damage both coach and bridge.

Whortleberries

In August the delicious little purple berries of the whortleberry can be found all over the moor, particularly on the drier slopes which the plant prefers. Until the early days of this century it was an annual tradition for the men, women and children of the villages around the moor to go together to good 'hurt'-gathering areas and spend days at a time harvesting the crop. It was possible for one person to pick as much as would fill three two-gallon buckets in a day. Add that to the fact that hundreds of people would be picking in each area, and one has to conclude that whortleberries are far less common than they once were. These days out on the moor were regarded as holidays by the villagers, although many needed the money they gained from the sale of the fruit. Crossing describes the idyllic nature of the job:

It is a picnic of the most unconventional character, and given sunny skies there is music in it from beginning to end. The picker leaves all his cares behind him – they are usually not very weighty ones – and gives himself up to the matter that has called him to the moor. The more youthful of the party are in high spirits, and the merry prattle of the children is heard all through the livelong day. And Nature comes forward to add to the pleasing sounds. An unseen songster carols overhead, and the stream sings to you from below. With all this ringing in your ears you scramble over grey boulders that the whortleberry plants partly hide, or take your ease upon some patch of short turf, hemmed in by tall bracken. By-and-by the sun tells the gatherers it is time to start upon their homeward way, and with well-filled baskets they turn their faces towards the village that lies beyond the hill over which the evening shadows are fast creeping.

(William Crossing, *A Dartmoor Worker*)

Autumn

Combestone Tor

In the middle distance is Huccaby, with Bellever Tor behind and Longaford Tor and Higher White Tor on the horizon.

This provides a good illustration of the way the granite tors of Dartmoor have weathered into strange shapes. The horizontal and vertical joints, which are characteristic of the structure of granite, have allowed frost to enter the cracks and continual freezing and thawing have in time levered one block away from another. Many of these blocks remain, standing separately, but many have fallen, thus creating the clitter that lies around the base of many tors.

Reaves in the Dart valley

At first this seems to be simply a view of the Dart valley with Yar Tor and Corndon Tor behind; but look more closely at the hillside below them. You can see a number of lines running parallel and straight up the hill. These low walls, which are called reaves, are at least 3000 years old. Together they form a total and extremely regular system of land division covering much of the moor. In fact Dartmoor has the largest surviving prehistoric field systems in the whole of Europe.

Recent survey and excavation work by Sheffield University has revealed much information about reaves, hitherto little understood. Perhaps their main significance lies in the size of the pattern and its regularity; a society whose land tenure was so carefully organized, must itself have been complex and sophisticated in ways which unfortunately we can only guess at.

A pony amongst the gorse and bracken

A strawberry roan pony enjoys the early autumn sun with never a thought for the hard days ahead. Pretty though it is, the colour of this pony indicates that it is not a pure-bred Dartmoor for these are normally dark brown. Indeed, hardly any of the ponies that run wild on the moor are pure-bred Dartmoors. During the First World War Shetland stallions were introduced to the moor and allowed to breed with Dartmoors to produce a smaller pony for use in the coal mines. Most of those seen on the moor today are the result of this cross-breeding. It is said that these 'scrub ponies' unfortunately lack the great stamina and survival ability of the true native Dartmoor pony. •

Heather

Heather in flower stretching in a purple sheet across particular areas of Dartmoor is the herald of autumn. The perfume in the air on a warm September day lingers long after as a palpable memory.

In earlier centuries heather was cut for bedding, thatching, basket making and fuel. It still has an important economic value as grazing for moorland stock.

Prehistoric stone row

This stone row stands on Hurston Ridge not far from the edge of Fernworthy Forest. There are about seventy such rows still existing, built about 3000 years ago by prehistoric inhabitants of Dartmoor. The rows vary considerably in size and pattern. Some are single, some double (as this one) and some treble. In length they vary from 165 feet to just over 2 miles and in height too some only just poke above the turf while some have stones of more than eight feet. Their orientation seems to be random.

This particular double row measures 472 feet with a gap of approximately 6 feet down the middle. There are fifty pairs of stones, some standing a good deal higher than others. At its lower end is a blocking stone and at its higher end a cairn. Many of the rows are similarly associated with a cairn or kist (burial chamber) and from this we can draw one firm conclusion about these mysterious stone rows; they were monuments which formed part of the rituals of death and burial of the prehistoric people of Dartmoor.

Rowan

With the scarlet berries come the warm dry days of early September. The berries are sour eaten raw but make a good tart jelly for seasoning meat. The birds, of course, appreciate them as they are, and it is through the digestive system of birds that rowan seeds are distributed, often leading to germination of rowans on crags and in crevices of tors.

Fly agaric

A delight special to autumn is coming across an unexpected scatter of fungi. Many of these are edible, but a few are highly poisonous. As its appearance suggests, the Fly Agaric is one of the latter. With its bright red cap and white spots, it is the archetypal toadstool of children's picture books. Look out for it in pine forests and birch woods.

Fairy clubs and giant polypore

Fungi are among the few plants which have no green pigment (chlorophyll) to enable them to make their own food as other plants do from carbon dioxide and water. They have to live off food made by other plants, or other organic matter. This is why many can be found on trees.

These two species illustrate how diverse in shape, size and colour fungi can be. But this is only the beginning! There are hundreds of types of fungi which are microscopic in size such as the mould on stale bread, while at the other end of the scale is the dry rot fungus with its yards and yards of tendrils (or hyphae) or the giant puffball which can measure over 1 foot across.

Moreover, what we think of as mushrooms or toadstools are only a part of the fungus – the reproductive part or fruiting body, as it is called. The main part of the plant – the hypha – is usually hidden in the ground, or tree, or rotting stump or cowpat where it grows. Sometimes, upon looking closely underneath the fruiting body, you can see the tangle of very fine threads which are the hypha.

The fruiting bodies produce not seeds, but spores, and in vast quantities. A fungus with a 2 inch wide cap, for example, will produce about 8000 million spores!

Autumn leaves

Beech leaves play a vivid part in the drama of autumn colours – first yellow, then golden and finally a bright foxy brown. The bark is normally smooth and grey, but the splendid mature beech trees in this wood (in the Bovey valley) are well covered by moss which likes the damp and shady conditions provided by the beech's dense leaf canopy.

Canoes on the River Dart

From New Bridge downstream, the River Dart is licensed for canoeing. It is a popular stretch with enough 'white water' between New Bridge and Holne Bridge for some national as well as local competitions to be held. The canoeing season lasts for the four months of winter – November to February.

Trendlebere Down

The stream hidden in the bottom of this narrow coombe runs directly to the River Bovey below Hisley Bridge. Here the colours of autumn are softer than elsewhere; the brown of the bracken is mixed and muted by the strong evergreen of gorse. The birch trees are pure pale gold; some have lost their leaves, and their silvery bark shines out sharply.

Birch trees are the advance guard of spreading woodland; provided man does not interfere and new saplings escape notice by grazing animals, this slope will in another thirty years be taken over by birch, hazel, willow and sapling beech and oak.

The foreground area has been bought by the National Park Authority, for it is a popular informal picnic site and viewpoint.

Slotted post

Common on Dartmoor farms (look out particularly along footpaths) are gateposts from pre-Industrial-Revolution days. Farmers would stop a gateway using wooden poles jammed between granite posts hewn to take the ends of the poles. The opposite post to this has inverted 'L'-shaped slots to the edge of the face, so that the end of the pole can be dropped in and lifted out easily.

Higher Uppacott, Poundsgate

Here is a charming traditional Dartmoor longhouse; indeed, it is such a good example of its type that in 1978 the National Park Committee took the opportunity to buy it when it came on the market.

Dartmoor longhouses are, by definition, long in plan with the living quarters at one end and the cattle shippon at the other, separated only by a cross-passage. All are built of granite and most date in their present form from the fourteenth century to the early seventeenth, although the pattern dates back to Saxon times. From the smoke-blackened rafters in Uppacott's roof we know that the fires were lit on a simple hearth and the smoke drifted up and out through the crevices in the thatch high above. By the late seventeenth century most farmers had got around to building chimneys and an upper storey in the lofty roof space.

Longhouses are as much a part of Dartmoor's landscape as the tors. In the recent past a few have been irredeemably altered in character, mainly by large windows replacing the old small ones – an inevitable consequence of the modern expectation of well-lit houses.

Beehives at Vitifer

During August and September when the heather is in bloom, beekeepers from many parts of Devon bring their hives on to the moor so the bees can harvest the rich nectar. This transhumance takes place in the evening and early night when the bees have returned to their hives. The beekeeper blocks the hive entrance to keep the bees in and perhaps lightly nails the parts of the hive together, though taking care to ensure adequate ventilation. He then takes the hives to his customary September spot and unblocks the entrance to the hive. The bees are likely to be thoroughly annoyed by all the jolting, but as it is probably nearly dark by this time they are not so keen to pour out of the hive seeking a painful revenge!

The next day they settle down to the business of collecting nectar and may be left for two to three weeks until the flowering is over. Heather honey is stiff and dark with a marvellous distinctive taste which makes it prized (and priced!) above all other honeys.

Ploughed field

On the far side of this field the River Teign flows, marking the boundary of the National Park below Bridford and Christow. The field has been newly tilled for winter wheat.

St Pancras Church, Widecombe-in-the-Moor

Widecombe is a tiny village set in the wide East Webburn valley of fields and farms, with moorland and tors on either side. The church is characteristic of moorland churches – built of granite with pinnacles at the four corners of the tower. It is, indeed, a particularly splendid example; the tower is 135 feet high and the fine barrel roof is decorated with colourful and individual roof bosses. One of these shows the emblem of the tinners' guild – three rabbits with shared ears. It is believed that the tin miners of Widecombe paid for the building of the tower in the early 1500s to give thanks for their success and prosperity.

The logs in the foreground are destined for the fireplace! Not for the coming winter but the one following, for a year is necessary to season firewood.

Widecombe Fair

Tom Pearce, Tom Pearce, lend me your grey mare,
All along, down along, out along lee.
For I want to go to Widecombe Fair
With Bill Brewer, Jan Stewer, Peter Gurney,
  Peter Davey, Dan'l Whiddon, Harry Hawke,
Old Uncle Tom Cobley and all.

This song, first recorded and published in 1880 and now a national folk song, is what has made Widecombe Fair perhaps the most widely known of all country fairs. It is held on the second Tuesday of September, usually in mild autumnal sunshine. The great variety of stalls and activities include the sheep show, where local farmers bring various breeds of sheep to be judged, and a horse and pony show, also with a number of different classes according to breed. A gymkhana involves the riders and horses in all sorts of tricky but funny races. (Try cantering with an egg and spoon!) There is show jumping too and a display of heavy horses. Towards the end of the day is a grand parade of all prize-winning horses and ponies, led by Uncle Tom Cobley himself on a grey mare.

There are usually demonstrations of different rural skills, such as rick thatching. There is clay-pigeon shooting, pillow fights on a slippery pole, skittles and other games to try your hand at. You can watch the parade of fox hounds and the fancy dress and visit the young farmers' tent, the side shows and, of course, the many refreshment tents. In the evening many people stay on to round off the day with a drink in the pub and join the energetic traditional country dance.

Fernworthy Reservoir

This reservoir was built in the 1930s by Torquay Corporation. It is now managed by South West Water. The water from Fernworthy is piped into three storage reservoirs near Hennock. This was the last granite-faced dam to be built on Dartmoor and a few local people still remember working on its construction.

Underneath its waters, as well as Fernworthy Farm, are two old bridges which once crossed the South Teign river. One is a medieval clapper bridge and beside it is a little humpbacked bridge built centuries later. In the recent water shortages in Devon, when the reservoir's level dropped dramatically, these drowned but enduring relics of earlier times were revealed. Of the two the older simpler clapper bridge will doubtless survive the longer.

Fernworthy Forest

This delightful sylvan entrance of larch and beech into Fernworthy Forest belies the acres of sitka spruce which lie beyond. These conifers were planted in the 1930s, at about the same time as the completion of the reservoir, and now, fifty years later, the trees are mature and being felled and the forest is being replanted with a greater variety of species.

Several forest trails and a round-reservoir walk have been laid out jointly by the Forestry Commission, South West Water and the National Park Authority. These offer many points of interest, but of particular note is the marvellous variety of unusual lichen that flourish in the dark damp coniferous undergrowth.

Lichen

This hairy-looking individual commonly known as beard fungus is one of over 1500 species of lichen in the British Isles. Only in the middle of the last century was it discovered that they were not mosses as previously thought, but an extraordinary partnership between two quite distinct plants – a fungus and an alga growing together in close and harmonious relationship. The role of each partner is complex and not fully understood, but in general terms it seems that the alga is able to photosynthesize food while the fungus provides water and a structure and shelter from wind and sun. Each strand of this lichen is composed of an outer fungal skin with a stratum of algal cells just within.

Dartmoor is rich in lichens and for that we should be thankful for most lichens grow only where the air is pure; they are unable to survive when emissions of smoke and industrial gases pollute the air. In many parts of England such lichens as the beard fungi do not exist.

Round-up

In autumn the farmer collects his moorland ewes and brings them down into fields on the farm to be served by the ram, or more probably, several rams. The shortening of the days triggers off the breeding mechanism of sheep which in the farming calendar is called tupping. The ewe's reproductive cycle lasts eighteen days, and so within that period most of them will have been 'caught' if the rams are playing their part properly. The shepherd or farmer knows when the ram has served the ewe; a 'raddle' of paint is put on the ram between his front legs so he automatically leaves a mark on the back of all the ewes he has served.

Frost on meadow grass

A first heavy frost, warmed and melted by the morning sun, transforms the seeds of this meadow grass into a delicate natural chandelier.

A moorland village

Sheepstor, on the western side of Dartmoor, is dominated by the massive hump of a tor by the same name, the lower flank of which is shown on the right of this photograph. In the distance are Leather Tor and Sharpitor. Nearby, surrounded by mature conifer plantations, is Burrator Reservoir which supplies Plymouth.

The village itself is very small – only sixty or so inhabitants in the parish – and is still very largely a farming community. Its main feature is the granite church in typical Dartmoor style, surmounted by four crocketted pinnacles. Ancillary features are the lych gate, the cross, and in the churchyard the red granite tombstones of the first two white Rajahs of Sarawak. The astonishing connection between the moorland village of Sheepstor and this far-eastern land is described inside the church.

▲ BLACKBERRIES

▲ ROWANBERRIES

▼ ROSEHIPS

▼ SLOES

Berries

In this 'season of mists and mellow fruitfulness' the wild fruits catch our eye – the brilliant reds of hips and haws and the enticing gleam of ripe blackberries. But more important, the colours catch the eye of those birds which eat them and, in doing so, help the plant to disperse its seeds to other areas. Birds have good colour vision and find it easy to spot the reds and blacks of berries against twigs and leaves.

A number of the common berries range from mildly to deadly poisonous to man. Others, however, are not only edible but nutritious and delicious. Everyone knows about blackberries for jam, jellies and pies, but also elderberries, rowanberries and wild crab-apples make jellies, hips make a vitamin-rich cordial, sloes can be added to gin, and all make excellent red country wines.

The countryside around Dartmoor overflows with goodies and every year tons are lost: think of the countless blackberries, for example, that never get picked. But is it really all wasted? Many of the blackberries that are not gathered are eaten by birds, foxes, mice and other small animals. The rest become the food of such insects as wasps, flies, ladybirds and caterpillars, and, when finally quite rotten, wild yeasts, moulds and fungi. So nature never wastes and at the end of the year a tiny proportion of the seeds within these fruits will be in a situation favourable for germination and growth.

Harvest festival in Hennock Church

Harvest festival is one of the main celebrations of the rural ecclesiastical year. Country churches look their best, decorated with flowers, fruit and grains of autumn, while shafts of golden September sun pierce the stained-glass windows. The harvest supper is a great occasion of good fellowship.

Throwleigh village centre

This converted barn, part of the complex of farm buildings which originally served Throwleigh Barton, dominates one side of the square at Throwleigh. A proposal some time ago to demolish it and replace it with two modern houses was, thankfully, not carried out. This gave the National Park planners a chance to work closely with a local builder and to guide and encourage him to achieve a development which has not only helped to keep one of Dartmoor's attractive, traditional buildings, but has almost certainly enhanced the appearance of Throwleigh's square.

Relic of the copper industry

Wheal Betsy was one of two important Dartmoor copper mines, both in Mary Tavy. This is the engine house, one of only a few surviving on Dartmoor, but like hundreds that still pepper the Cornish landscape. During the first half of the nineteenth century Wheal Betsy produced thousands of tons of copper and also considerable quantities of arsenic, lead and silver.

The engine house is now owned and maintained by the National Trust.

Rabbiting

Although the rabbit population is much smaller than it was before myxamatosis was introduced, rabbits are numerous enough to be a nuisance to some farmers and are hunted to reduce their numbers and to provide a tasty meal.

Rabbits can be shot (but not trapped, which is now illegal) or caught at night with lights and dogs. Here a ferret was used. All the holes have nets placed across their entrance and a trained ferret is put down the burrow. The rabbits, in their terror to get away, fly out of the hole and are caught in the net. They are then rapidly dispatched.

Pony drift

For most of the year the ponies on Dartmoor are left to themselves, to go where they will and eat what they can. It seems a free and wild life, at least within the confines of the herd and its territory. But once a year comes the time of reckoning when the farmers and others who own them get together to round them up and claim their own.

There are several of these 'drifts' on different days at the beginning of October, each covering a particular area and its herds. It is a peculiarly Dartmoor occasion, when neighbouring farming families work together (as used to be the practice everywhere at haytime and harvest) to bring the ponies in. Once they are down and secure in the yards or the fields of the farm to which they belong, they are sorted out; the mares go back to the moor along with the filly foals, but the colts take their chance at markets the following week.

The River Plym

On a damp autumn day with the sun just struggling through the mist, 'since golden October declined into sombre November', the Plym pursues its rocky course above Cadover Bridge. In the distance is Shaugh Moor and the road leading away from Cadover Bridge to Beatland Cross.

Salmon leaping

Salmon normally leave the sea and swim up river to the reddes (or spawning grounds) in autumn. They leave the sea plump and sleek with bright scales, but as soon as they enter the fresh water they stop eating altogether and in the course of their progress up river become gradually thinner and darker. They wait in pools below the weirs until heavy rain on the hills creates a torrent which enables them to leap over the weir. They then continue upstream to the reddes – beds of gravel – where they will spawn. This will probably involve another wait for winter to advance as they need the water to drop below a certain temperature. Then the hen fish makes a hollow in the gravel with her tail and there lays the eggs which are fertilized immediately by the cock salmon. They cover the eggs, and, by now very dark and thin, die fairly soon, having completed their purpose and life cycle.

The eggs hatch in the spring and the young salmon stay in the river for the first two or three years before swimming down river to the ocean to live out the next phase of their lives.

Parke house and estate

For more than two centuries Parke was the home of the Hole family. Then in 1974, when Major Hole died at the age of ninety-one, he left his house and land to the National Trust. The house was built in the 1820s, but although characteristic of the gracious Georgian architecture of that period, it is not of sufficient interest or size to be opened to the public. The National Trust, therefore, sought a tenant and in 1979 Dartmoor National Park Authority left County Hall in Exeter and moved into this lovely house on the edge of Dartmoor.

The estate is 138 acres of meadow and woodland, leat and pool, with the River Bovey and the course of the old Moretonhampstead railway line running through it. New paths added to the existing ones have made a delightful variety of walks, all open to the public. The farm buildings and land are occupied by a rare breeds collection (Parke Rare Breeds Farm) open to visitors from spring until autumn. An Interpretation Centre, tea rooms and an orchard picnic area complete the facilities which offer a pleasant and interesting afternoon out.

Lee Moor

Within the extreme south-west corner of Dartmoor is a white wasteland where china clay is won from this and other pits. Clay is one of the products of decomposed granite; millions of years ago the feldspar in the granite was altered by hot acidic gases in the ground to kaolin (china clay). It is now an extremely valuable product for use in paints, chemicals, medicines, engineering products and so on. Not much of it is used to make china teasets any longer!

This particular pit is over 300 feet deep and the deposit of kaolin exists for a further 300 feet and more below the pit bottom. The greatest problem for clay companies is where to dispose of the great quantities of sand that are left after the clay has been extracted. The white pyramids or terraces of waste sand are very carefully located, so as to spoil as little moorland as possible, and are eventually landscaped and grassed over.

The Dart valley

From Sharp Tor is this view over the Dart valley. To the centre right of the picture and not particularly prominent is Combestone Tor. Behind is the valley of the O Brook, with its humps, hollows, leat channels, wheelpits and 'buddles' – the intriguing remains of Henroost and Hooten Wheal mines. On the far left is Hangman's Pit, a deep mining gully, so named according to Crossing from the farmer who in the early nineteenth century hung himself after reputedly being swindled at market. It is a landscape full of stories!

Gorse

> When gorse is not in flower
> Kissing's out of fashion.

In fact it is just one species, common gorse, that flowers all the year round, even in midwinter. On Dartmoor cushions of western furze, which flowers only in high summer, are also present on many higher hillsides. Gorse fixes nitrogen, like clover, and its young shoots are edible into winter and early spring.

Young larch trees

Larches help to soften the hard, dark appearance of many of the conifer plantations on Dartmoor and in nearby valleys. They are deciduous conifers; in autumn when other conifers stay dark green the larch needles, by contrast, turn pale yellow and drop off. Separate male and female flowers grow on each tree and the fruit that develops is a light fairly small woody cone which hangs on long after the needles have dropped.

These young trees are in Fernworthy plantation. They will not perhaps yield as much as the more common sitka spruce, but nevertheless they will provide a durable timber particularly suitable for such outside use as fence posts and cladding.

Haytor Quarries and Tramway

Beyond Haytor Rocks are the quarries, long abandoned and now adding beauty and interest to the landscape.

Quarrying for granite on Dartmoor started only towards the end of the eighteenth century for previously the surface granite provided enough for local needs. But with the growth of towns large quantities were quarried and transported away.

At Haytor quarrying began sometime before 1820. Spurred on by winning a contract to supply the stone for the new London Bridge, Mr Templer, the quarry owner, built a tramway linking the quarries to the Stover Canal. The track was 8½ miles long and unusual in that the rails were of granite rather than metal. The wagons were drawn by horses aided by a primitive braking system on the downhill run. The quarry was busy from the 1820s for forty years or so. After that work was intermittent; the last job was the cutting of a war memorial for Exeter in 1919. Parts of the winding and lifting gear still remain and so does much of the tramway, at least on the moor, with a few well-hidden milestones.

Swallerton Gate

This solitary cottage below Hound Tor was once an inn or cider house in the days of wool prosperity on the moor. Beside it was a moorgate, one of many around the moor that kept the stock out of the lanes. The children of the cottage would rush to open and close the gate for passers-by, hoping to be thrown a penny in reward.

The name 'Swallerton' is a corruption of 'Swine Down' nearby.

Baling bracken

It is becoming more common these days to find bracken sold in garden centres as a mulch. In a very few places on Dartmoor (where the ground is sufficiently free of rocks) it is cut and baled as it turns brown in the autumn.

In previous centuries bracken was far more highly valued than it is now. It provided bedding in the cattle byres, sheep sheds and pig pens during the winter months. We know that it was once a valuable and much scarcer commodity as there existed a limit on how much each commoner could take. Nowadays there are Ministry grants for attempts to eradicate it!

Autumn churchyard

A favourite subject for reflection since writing began (and probably before) is the poetic parallel between the passing of man and the passing of the seasons. This picture of Chagford churchyard captures the gentle melancholy of seemly death and decay for both man and nature.

Grieve not that in the wintry air
Dead souls of summer days are seen;
Already blackened boughs prepare
The certain gift of next year's green.
(Hamilton Fyfe, 'Dead Leaves')

Castle Drogo

Completed in 1931, Castle Drogo is the only castle to be built in England in the twentieth century. It was built by a family called Drewe who founded the Home & Colonial Stores chain. The famous architect Edwin Lutyens designed it, but at times his ideas were in conflict with those of Julius Drewe, and his full design was never completed.

The choice of site is impressive, for Castle Drogo sits at the upper end of the Teign gorge with wide views to the moor. It is built of massive and yet marvellously intricate blocks of granite, and the gardens are formal but full of sweet-scented shrubs and flowers. It is a delightful place and one which visitors can now enjoy, since in 1974 the Drewe family donated it to the National Trust.

Hound Tor

An autumn mist hangs over the weird outline of Hound Tor. Not a wonder that Dartmoor people until fairly recently saw black dogs, packs of Whist Hounds, headless riders and other ghostly horrors looming up out of the mist. The Reverend Baring-Gould, turn-of-the-century Dartmoor devotee, claimed that its name was derived from 'the blocks on the summit, that have been weathered into forms resembling the heads of dogs peering over the natural battlements'.

Moorland peat

The upland plateaux are relatively flat and in many places the water cannot readily drain away. It is often hindered by the existence of a continuous and impermeable layer of iron (iron pan) normally about 10 inches below the surface. Because of this poor drainage and the very high rainfall, the ground becomes totally waterlogged. In these conditions the sphagnum moss, grasses and other plants do not decompose in the normal way when they die, but build up into peat, a fibrous mat of root and stem material, which itself acts as a natural sponge.

It was not always so on Dartmoor; peat formation through the millenia has fluctuated in response to changing climate. Depth of peat varies from a few inches to over 12 feet on the northern plateau, but evidence suggests that the peat is shrinking slowly.

The hollow in the lower picture is a shell hole, a result of the army's firing practice on parts of the high northern moor. There is some evidence that concentrated shelling has led to peat erosion; the R.S.P.B. is concerned that birds are discouraged from breeding in the affected areas.

Holne Moor Leat

This is one of two running leats on Holne Moor, not to mention several dry ones. It brings water from the O Brook to the Holy Brook above Buckfastleigh, a distance of 4½ miles. The water is then extracted further down the Holy Brook by the Buckfast Plating Company. Leats with running water are still in use as drinking water by both people and animals so it is important that they are not blocked or the banks broken down.

On the horizon, on the far side of the Dart valley are (from left to right) Yar Tor, Corndon Tor and Sharp Tor.

November Day

Deciduous, soft days are soon forgotten
When brown winds whip each branch and footprints freeze;
But as leaves layer down, rancid and rotten,
At last there is a vista through the trees
Through telescopic, true November
We view contours and crags unknown before–
And with last year's nostalgia remember
The field and cottage, valley and tor
The distant hills
Seem larger, clearer,
Nearer.

(Margaret Calloway, *Collected poems*, Dartington Poetry Press, 1984)

Windypost

On the slope of Whitchurch Common overlooking the Walkham valley, this cross stands solitary and prominent. In medieval times when the abbeys of Buckfast and Tavistock were among the largest landowners and farmers in Devon, they developed tracks across the moor for trading purposes. This cross is estimated to date from the fifteenth century and with others (some of which still stand) marked a track from Tavistock to Ashburton.

Bull's-eye stone

Beside the cross runs the Grimstone and Sortridge leat which was built in the mid-nineteenth century to bring water to the copper mines on farms of those names in the parish of Horrabridge on the western side of the moor. Just upstream from the cross in the lower leat wall is a stone with a 'bull's-eye', or 'inch hole', drilled through the granite to allow a fixed and small amount of water to be supplied to a branch leat which waters farms and fields around Sampford Spiney.

At this junction of nineteenth-century leat and fifteenth-century track, miners and monks toiled and travelled – separated by 400 years of change!

Wheelwright's form

This stone lies beside the ruins of a smithy which serviced the great nineteenth-century quarries in the area. The stone form was used for assembling the hub, spokes and rim of the wheel, and finally the red-hot iron tyre which was dropped outside the rim. Cold water was immediately thrown on to it, the iron tyre cooled rapidly, contracting into the wooden rim and encircling and holding the complete wheel in its 'iron grip'.

In the middle distance on the left-hand side of the picture is Vixen Tor, the tallest (at 52 feet) on Dartmoor.

The last beech leaf

The leaves of the beech hang on into late autumn, bright and brown. They eventually fall but still linger as dry papery leaves in odd corners where the wind has blown them or, as here, in other ground vegetation.

Guy Fawkes night at Hennock

Many villages organize a celebration on 5th November. The guy is burned on a huge pile of unwanted timber, rough branches, wrecked furniture and so on. On a smaller more controlled fire a lamb or 'ox' might be roasted with the juice dripping down and sizzling on the red embers below. And of course fireworks complete the evening for the particular delight of the younger children.

Rain cloud above Staple Tors

A cloud, heavy with rain, sweeps in from the west, as does most of the copious Dartmoor rainfall. The clouds hit the cold high ground, rise and, cooling rapidly, shed their load. Dartmoor's annual average rainfall is 60 inches, compared with below 40 inches for the rest of Devon (or, to take an extreme contrast, 92 inches at Princetown, 35 inches at Torquay!). There is an old saying about Dartmoor: 'Nine months winter and three months bad weather'.

Venford Reservoir

Away! the moor is dark beneath the moon,
Rapid clouds have drunk the last pale beam of even:
Away! the gathering winds will call the darkness soon
And profoundest midnight shroud the serene lights of heaven.

(P.B. Shelley, 'Stanzas – April 1814')

Winter

The Dewerstone

The towering cliff called the Dewerstone, the highest inland granite cliff in Devon, overlooks the Plym valley just above its junction with the River Meavy. At its highest (Devil's Rock) it is 170 feet and is a favourite route for climbers. In 1960 a climber on the Dewerstone discovered, wedged in a rock crevice, a prehistoric pottery mug, which although broken in two, was complete. It is now in Plymouth City Museum.

Frost

On a cold morning, in the words of the poet Ted Hughes, the leaves are 'fur-gloved with frost'. This is a woodland floor mosaic of creeping ivy, brambles and grass; green, white, brown and black.

Remains of a prehistoric hut circle on Shapley Common

This prehistoric house is one of at least 2000 remaining on Dartmoor from a distant past – about 2000 to 500 B.C. In those times, when the land above about 1600 feet was an open upland surrounded by forest and the climate was warmer than nowadays, it must have been an ideal place for the people to graze their cattle and even grow a few crops. By the number of hut circles remaining, it seems likely that they settled in some numbers and over a vast period of time.

The huts or houses had thick walls of granite and conical roofs of turf or heather and wood, each supported by a central post. Inside some were partly paved with hearths, and some had porches; one even had wooden planks lining the inside of the walls. They varied from 9 to 33 feet in diameter, the larger ones having an inner row of posts to help support the roof.

Muck-spreading

Valuable dung goes back to the fields, scattered by a rotary spreader behind the tractor. The invention of this particular device was one of those, along with the combine harvester, the forage harvester and the milking machine, which has hugely reduced the laborious side of farming as it was until after the Second World War.

Muck-spreading before then entailed manually loading the manure on to a cart which was drawn to the field. The farmer would stop the cart at regular intervals, pulling the manure off the back of it into small heaps. A few days later, when it had dried off a bit, he would go back and scatter the heaps. A time-consuming and strenuous process – the only thing which has not changed in the meanwhile is the smell!

Tree planting at Lustleigh

From November until late March is the time to plant trees, and the National Park Authority encourages trees in the landscape by supplying free saplings, planting many itself and maintaining its own woods.

The management of the Commons of Dartmoor

The heart of Dartmoor – 100 000 acres of high moorland – is legally common land. Common land is that 'held subject to the rights of others'; those rights (of named individuals) on most of the commons of England and Wales are to graze and take wood, stone, gravel and peat for domestic purposes.

Until the end of the nineteenth century, when the hardy breeds of cattle (Galloways) and sheep (Scotch Blackface) were introduced to Dartmoor, all the livestock was taken off the moor during winter because the local breeds were not hardy enough to withstand the severity of a Dartmoor winter. This meant that they had the shelter and grass of in-bye fields, and it also meant

that no farmer could keep more stock on the common during the summer than he could overwinter in his fields. Such practice gave the moorland vegetation a chance to recover. This arrangement for regulating the use of the commons by the commoners has long since ceased to be effective. Consequently the moorland vegetation is to a large extent unmanaged and livestock in some cases not well looked after.

In 1985, after ten years of effort by the National Park Authority and the Dartmoor Commoners' Association, the Dartmoor Commons Act was passed by Parliament. This Act sets up the mechanism for better control of the way the common land of Dartmoor is used, both by commoners (those with common rights) and the visiting public. It thus seeks to resolve the existing free-for-all involving 1500 commoners and 55 owners of 93 commons, visited by 8 million people a year.

The Act creates a Commoners' Council, composed of equal numbers of elected members from the four quarters of the Dartmoor Commons, twenty in all, with representatives from the National Park Authority, the Duchy of Cornwall, other owners and a vet. The Council has the power to enforce good husbandry by individual commoners, and to control the numbers of cattle, sheep and ponies on any one common.

The Act also legalizes access for walkers and riders who want to enjoy the moorland commons. It enables byelaws to be made to help control anti-social and anti-country-code behaviour where necessary, and requires the National Park Authority to protect land from access for good reasons, and temporarily, when necessary.

The Dartmoor Commons Act is unique in this country as a device for controlling the use of land, livestock and recreation. One measure of its success will be when observers of livestock on the moor, sometimes upset at the condition of ponies and other animals in the winter will no longer have cause to complain.

The western flank

This dramatic view of the western edge of the moor is from Great Mis Tor. Across the Walkham valley and behind Cocks Hill is Tavy Cleave, overlooked by Ger Tor. On the skyline are Brat Tor, left, and Great Links Tor, right. It is noticeable that most of this side of Dartmoor lacks the heather sward of the eastern side.

Buzzard

Dartmoor's largest bird of prey is the buzzard. Normally it is seen from below, when with wings outspread it soars in wide circles, hovering in the thermal updraughts to scan for movement on the ground. Then it pounces. Its prey is usually small mammals or beetles or occasionally other small birds. Rabbits formed a large part of buzzards' diets until their almost complete extermination by myxamatosis badly affected buzzard numbers. Since then, thankfully, the buzzard population has gradually re-established itself and on Dartmoor one can often see several pairs at a time. As nesting sites they tend to prefer tall trees; consequently most plantations on Dartmoor and several isolated trees contain buzzards' nests.

The River Bovey

In rivers there is wisdom, quiet, release:
Wherever there are rivers there is peace.

(James Walker, 'Peace')

Heather management

This picture on Hameldown is a striking illustration of how different stages of growth determine the appearance of heather moorland. The heather on the right is younger than that on the left as it was burned (swaled) more recently. The path acted as a natural firebreak and was made use of for that purpose by the swalers.

It is important that heather is burned periodically. It is in fact a small shrub which lives for about twenty-five to thirty years. If a whole heather sward is allowed to reach its full age and die, it will do so all at once and regeneration is weak. This lets in other invasive plants – purple moor grass and bracken – and once established they oust the heather. Also, if heather is left until it is old and leggy when it is finally burned, or inadvertently catches fire, the heat generated may be so great that the roots themselves are killed along with any heather seeds in the soil.

It is equally important not to burn too frequently; for decades now it has been accepted that overburning can cause a decline in heather. The best situation, and one which the National Park Authority, Duchy of Cornwall and Commoners are working towards, is one where a mosaic of heather swards of different ages exist. The breeding birds prefer this variety, farmers prefer it for their grazing animals, it helps to prevent accidental or wilful spread of fire, and overall it ensures the continuation of healthy and beautiful heather moorland.

Prehistoric settlement in the Walkham valley

The valleys of southern Dartmoor boast some marvellous collections of huts and pounds dating from the second millenium B.C. In this valley about 150 houses have been counted. The people living here were farmers, pasturing small herds of beef and dairy cattle and sheep upon the open land of the moor.

They grew crops, including grain for bread, and had access to pottery (not made locally), flint and chert tools and bronze knives and other implements. Whether or not the bronze tools were made from tin (and copper) gathered and smelted on Dartmoor is still a much-debated matter. There is no evidence of prehistoric smelting, yet it would seem unlikely that, being part of a metal-working culture, these people did not recognize and exploit that immensely rich resource all around them.

Kistvaen at Roundy Pound

About three-quarters of a mile upstream from Postbridge is Roundy Pound, a prehistoric pound (but rebuilt and used in historic times) which has within it a few hut circles and, close to the wall, this sepulchral relic. A kistvaen is a stone chest made of four slabs of stone and covered by a wide flat capstone. There are nearly 100 known to exist on the moor today. They were built in the second millenium B.C. as tombs and probably housed only one body (either trussed up or its ashes) unlike the chambered cairns or barrows which accommodated a sequence of burials. The kists often had a circle of stone around them as this one has, and probably would have been covered by a mound of earth or small stones. They varied a good deal in size, this being one of the largest.

Cairn on Hameldown

Cairns are artificial mounds built as burial sites in prehistoric times. Those found on Dartmoor are invariably round, almost always comprised of granite and many were sited on hill tops – some indeed enclosed and covered a natural hill-top tor. Many of them would cover a kistvaen into which the ashes of the corpse were placed in a clay pot. Sometimes the ashes were placed in a pit sunk beneath the ground (occasionally paved) under the cairn. In other cases the stones have simply been heaped over the site of the cremation.

Brentor Church

The tiny church of St Michael de Rupe stands on a prominent cone-shaped hill on the western edge of the moor. It can be seen from most parts of western Devon and well over the Tamar into Cornwall. It was built within a prehistoric earthwork. The hill is an example of a long-dead volcanic plug, a number of which lie at the edge of the Dartmoor granite mass. Its steep ascent is by a flight of granite steps which the National Park Authority built to prevent further erosion of the track.

Blackbrook

Partly spanned by a clapper bridge, the Blackbrook glides along on a cold winter afternoon with the chimneys of Princetown prison just visible through the trees. This stream rises on the flanks of Black Dunghill nearly 2 miles north and continues for another 2½ miles or so before joining the West Dart below Two Bridges.

Bellever Tor

Bellever Tor stands proud of the forest that now virtually surrounds it, the trig point marking a height of 1456 feet. This is the view to the east, with Hameldown, Haytor and Rippon Tor on the horizon.

When the horizontal joints in the granite are particularly close together as they are on Bellever it indicates that this was near the original top of the granite mass that underlies Dartmoor.

Bellever Forest was planted by the Forestry Commission in 1930, the same year in which they took over management from the Duchy of most afforested moorland areas on Dartmoor. Before the 1930s Bellever was the venue every May for the last hunt meet of the season – Bellever Day, as it was known – in which the Dartmoor hunts united, a very popular event. There were side stalls, villagers selling food and drink, picnics, organized races for people on foot and on horse, but most important, there were hundreds of Dartmoor people (Crossing estimated over 1000 in 1901) who had walked or ridden from their farms and villages all over the moor for this colourful communal event.

Snow on the hills

During winter months the hills of Dartmoor frequently lie snow-covered while the lowlands escape with a mere dusting, or none at all. The distant green and sunlit fields are in the South Hams.

The East Dart River

The river exposes the granite bedrock lying just beneath the thin surface covering of peat and grass.

Soldiers in training

Since 1877, when the army set up camp for six weeks' artillery practice in Okehampton Park, Dartmoor has regularly been used for military training. By 1895 a permanent camp had been built and the War Office was renting the whole of the northern quarter of the moor. In 1900 it bought Willsworthy Manor and made a rifle range there, but at the outbreak of the Second World War virtually all northern Dartmoor was commandeered as a firing range and training and firing also took place in many other parts.

After the war the Government declared that it needed over 70 000 acres, from 52 000 of which the public was to be totally excluded. The outcry that this caused led to a reduction to 33 000 acres with the public excluded only when firing was taking place. Since then, apart from the hardening of previously rough tracks in 1956, there has not been much change until recently when the area around Cramber Tor was taken over for dry training (no firing), new rifle ranges were built at Willsworthy, and at Okehampton Camp, an unfortunate eyesore, structural consolidations were made to the temporary sheds.

Military observation post

This is one of the inevitable results of the army's use of Dartmoor as a training area.

The Falklands Memorial at Merrivale Quarry

After the Falklands War in 1982 this memorial was commissioned in memory of the ships and men involved in that conflict. The granite was quarried at Merrivale, sent away to be engraved and returned to the quarry for reassembly and completion. It was transported to Port Stanley, but while still on board ship was damaged by a fire. Two replacement stones had to be cut at Merrivale and shipped out.

Highland cattle on Butterdon Hill

The long pointed horns, shaggy coat and look of thick-set strength all combine to give this highland cow a primaevally wild and untamed appearance. She is, in fact, much more docile than her appearance suggests, which is just as well since several herds of this breed of cattle live on Dartmoor. Their main characteristic is their extreme hardiness; they can survive severe weather and keep themselves alive on the roughest vegetation when others would quickly die. Indeed, they are more likely to die if penned up and housed.

Highlanders come in exotic colours – black, red, yellow, silver dun and white. This cow is silver dun and is in a largely silver dun herd (or fold) of about 200 who since 1941 have roamed the moor above Bittaford.

Boundary stone on Hameldown

All over Dartmoor are boundary or 'bond' stones marking the edges of different places – the Forest of Dartmoor, parishes, water-catchment areas, tin workings and, above all, private land ownership. This particular stone marks the limits of the lands in the Haytor/Hameldown area of the Duke of Somerset, a large nineteenth-century landowner.

Soft rush

In the dry but very cold winter of 1985–6 all the moorland pools completely froze and anything poking above the snow was seared by an icy breath of east wind, as happened to this soft rush. It is one of the plants very much at home in Dartmoor's waterlogged and acid peat. Its long pithy rushes used to be picked, carefuly dried and woven into mats and small baskets by Dartmoor people.

Granite cut by feather and tare

The granite lying on the surface of the moor has traditionally been called moorstone. Until the early nineteenth century when quarrying became commercially viable, it normally supplied the needs of the local people for general building purposes (houses, barns, field walls) and more specific purposes, such as gate posts, grind stones, wheelwright forms, troughs and so on.

The age-old method of splitting granite consisted of making a groove along the required line in the granite with a bolster and simply deepening it until (it was hoped!) the granite split along that line. However, granite has its own internal stresses and the outcome was sometimes a split in the wrong place. At the beginning of the 1800s a new and more dependable method was adopted. Holes about 4 inches deep were drilled by hand (rotating a tapered chisel) in a row and then a wedge and two half-round bars placed in each. The wedges were then tapped in sequence until the rock split along the line of the holes. Here, as in countless places on the moor, can be seen the result of a rock split by this method.

Princetown

The prison at Princetown was the reason for Princetown's continuing existence in this high, cold, wet exposed spot. The village itself was founded in the 1790s by an enthusiastic agricultural improver called Sir Thomas Tyrwhitt. The climate and soil conditions were (as Tyrwhitt should have realized) hostile to his ambitions of growing corn, flax and other crops and the little community was an economic failure. To save it, in 1805 Tyrwhitt suggested that it would be a highly suitable place to build a prison to accommodate some of the French prisoners from the Napoleonic Wars who were then in appallingly overcrowded conditions in ships anchored at Plymouth. So the prison came to be built.

The subsequent story of this imposing complex of buildings is varied and fascinating. For a short period it was taken over by the British Patent Naphtha Company for the manufacture of naphtha from peat. In 1850 it became a prison again after thirty-four years of virtual disuse, but this time it was for civil criminals. About 600 category B criminals are now housed there, with a staff of about 250. The two blocks in this photograph are what remains of the seven original blocks of the old war prison. The majority of houses in the village are prison officers' houses and most employment is associated with the prison.

Cottage at Hennock

On a snowy December night this cottage is the epitome of warmth, welcome and good cheer. Its walls of cob, the thatched roof and relatively small, irregularly placed windows are instantly recognizable features of a traditional Devon dwelling.

A winter walk

A walk in the winter over Dartmoor tempts fewer people than at other times of year. That indefatigable walker William Crossing (who once walked for twenty-eight hours without stopping, missing two nights sleep!) expressed it: 'It is possible to walk . . . for a whole day, and never see a sign of recent occupancy or cultivation, or to meet with a single person on the journey. Nothing but great stretches of moorland, rushing rivers, and lofty hills capped with fantastic granite tors can be seen . . . (from *Amid Devonia's Alps.*)

Crossing wrote this in 1888, but until very recently the same has held true, and even today a winter walk on Dartmoor by oneself, or with a few friends, can generate that unique feeling of exhilaration and peace.

In his famous *Guide to Dartmoor* (1909) he advises about bogs, mists, Scotch cattle and burning peat. About equipment and clothes he says 'all that the visitor needs to take with him on his rambles over the moor is a stout stick, a sandwich case and a pocket compass'. Today we would add a 2½ inch scale map, warm and waterproof garments and good boots. But Crossing does in fact go on to mention boots: 'If, when he (the visitor) reaches his destination at night, his boots are wet, let him fill them with oats . . . The grain absorbs the moisture and swells, and when shaken out in the morning, the boots will be found to have preserved their shape.' Winter walking nowadays is certainly easier!

Volunteers erecting a signpost

During the winter the National Park Rangers have time to turn their attention to the maintenance of the 500-plus miles of public rights of way within the National Park. They are sometimes helped by volunteers, as in this photograph where a small group of Duke of Edinburgh Award volunteers have just finished putting up a footpath signpost.

The hunt

Five hunts cover Dartmoor on a regular basis, each tending to keep to their own country and meeting during the season two or three times a week. To be a hunt subscriber and ride with the hounds costs a little over £100 a year and a hunt subscriber who attends regularly will eventually probably be nominated to become a member. This is an honorary status marked by buttons worn on the hunting coat. However, many people are happy to follow on foot or, as far as possible, in their cars, for a small donation.

Each hunt has its own kennels and although you may see, perhaps, seventeen couples (they are always counted in couples), there may well be as many again back in the kennels. The hunt here is meeting at Two Bridges.

Shooting

With slaught'ring guns th' unweary fowler roves,
When frosts have whitened all the naked groves;
Where doves in flocks the leafless trees o'ershade,
And lonely woodcocks haunt the watery glade.
He lifts the tube and levels with his eye;
Straight a short thunder breaks the frozen sky:
Oft' as in airy rings they skim the heath,
The clam'rous plovers feel the leaden death:
Oft' as the mounting larks their notes prepare,
They fall and leave their little lives in air.

(Alexander Pope, 'Windsor Forest')

When Pope was writing at the beginning of the eighteenth century, game, both feathered and furred, was far more plentiful than it is today. The general spread of guns in the nineteenth-century countryside, followed by the loss of habitat and use of pesticides and herbicides in the twentieth century, have reduced to pitiful proportions the many species that once thronged the valleys and hills.

The still figure here with gun loosely held but ready for action is waiting for nothing more rare than a common wood pigeon, fat from feasts of ivy berries.

Drift lane at Postbridge

From the drift lane the tiny fleck of blue betrays where the East Dart River meanders down towards Postbridge.

Drift lanes are designed to help collect the moorland stock at times when the animals need to be brought off the moor. Most are found between field walls on the borders of Dartmoor, forming a funnel with a gate at the bottom. Stock can easily be driven into the wide end and then through the gate left open at the far end and so caught. The drift lanes are as old as the boundaries on either side of them, mostly medieval. The Postbridge drift lane, however, is much more modern.

As the nineteenth-century newtakes gradually enclosed this part of the moor, this lane was left as a passage through them, linking the tenant farms in the East Dart valley with the high moor. Eventually the end of the lane was cut off by even bigger newtakes, extending further into the moor, but perhaps by this time the practice of driving stock up on to the moors had discontinued, particularly since the Duchy of Cornwall had allowed this part of the Dart valley to become almost entirely enclosed by private tenants.

Today the drift lane provides an attractive and easy way for walkers from Postbridge to reach the upper East Dart and beyond.

Haytor from Blackingstone

The twin peaks of Haytor form an impressive part of the view from the Blackingstone ridge, particularly when they appear to float above a dense mist in the Wray valley. This morning 'mist in the valley' presages a fine day ahead.

Landscape under snow

I love to see when leaves depart
The clear anatomy arrive.
Winter, the paragon of art
Which kills all forms of life and feeling
Save what is pure and will survive.
(Roy Campbell, *Collected Poems*)

Moorland road

The snow reflects the blue of the sky as a strong unclouded sun begins to melt the roadside drifts.

The ammil

There occasionally occurs on Dartmoor a phenomenon known as the 'ammil'. In certain weather conditions each leaf, twig, bush and rock on the moor is entirely coated with a thin layer of ice. It is an extraordinary and beautiful sight accompanied, when a breeze gets up, by a sound like hundreds of tiny melodious cymbals, made by the tinkle of the little icicles knocking together. Sometimes it happens in isolated spots and sometimes, more rarely, over large areas of Dartmoor. In 1947 this latter happened and is referred to as the 'Great Ammil'.

Henry Williamson, in his famous book *Tarka the Otter*, describes such a scene poetically:

> When the sun, like an immense dandelion, looked over the light-smitten height of Cosdon Beacon, Tarka was returning along a lynch, or rough trackway to the river. The grasses, the heather, the lichens, the whortleberry bushes, the mosses, the boulders – everything in front of the otter vanished as though drowned or dissolved in a luminous strange sea. The icy casings of leaves and grasses and blades and sprigs were glowing and hid in a mist of sun-fire.

Mining gullies on Headland Warren

Tin mining on Dartmoor experienced three boom periods. This open-cast system of extraction typifies the second phase which occurred from the fifteenth to the early seventeenth centuries. The lodes of tin were traced up the hillsides and excavated with pick and shovel. Some of these earthworks must have been 80 feet deep or more. Whenever possible water would be diverted and brought in leats to wash away the lighter rock and expose the ore. But at these particular workings (or gerts, as they are called locally) well up the hillside it is difficult to see how water power could have been used. These gerts were probably deepened and extended by the operators of the nineteenth-century shaft-mining complex at Vitifer in the valley just below.

Gorse and snow

A gorse bush bows under the weight of snow while a leaden sky, heavy with the promise of more snow, bears down upon the horizon.

Winter feeding

The daily rations of hay are loaded and fed to the stock. However, Dartmoor farmers now tend to make silage rather than hay. Well-fermented silage is greatly enjoyed by the animals and contains more food value than hay. The small fields of Dartmoor's valley farmland are not always suitable for the big machinery necessary to make silage. In many parts of the country hedges and walls have been bulldozed away to accommodate the new machinery but on Dartmoor and in other national parks, where such features are held to be a vital part of the landscape, farmers are compensated for not destroying the pattern of small fields. So hay will continue to be part of the diet of at least some of the cattle and sheep on the moor. It is also certainly easier and pleasanter to handle in small quantities and to use as feed in small sheds.

Waterfall on the East Dart

On the upper reaches of the East Dart are some small waterfalls which after rain become a furious torrent of sound. Dartmoor's peat is like a massive sponge capable of holding huge amounts of water. But in the winter the peat is more often than not already in a state of saturation and further excessive rainfall cannot be absorbed. When this happens the rivers rise rapidly, perhaps several feet in an hour; on the River Dart are recorded rises of 7 feet before the waters began to subside. On these occasions the water is an ominous brown, stained by the peat it has passed over.

Icicles

All along the edges of the stream King Frost does marvellous work. Where the joyous flood dances and splashes, showering tiny sheets of spray up on its banks, Frost deftly catches the water wherever it falls and transforms it into his own crystals. Each grass blade is set in a glass case; each clover leaf is a crozier of crystal; every twig is inch thick in stainless ice . . .

(Beatrice Chase, *The Heart of the Moor*)

Ash-house at West Coombe

These little round buildings can be found on about thirty-five Dartmoor farms, nearly all on the eastern side of the moor. They were built to take the ash cleaned out daily from the farmhouse hearth. The double benefit of this was that, first, any still-glowing embers in the ash were safely stored out of risk to the farmhouse thatch, and secondly, the ash, perhaps mixed with droppings from roosting chickens, formed a potent nitrogenous fertilizer for the acid Dartmoor soil.

The corbelled roof of this ash-house had a protective covering of turf but this died after the drought summers of 1976 and 1977 and the rain began to wash out the mortar between the stones. It would probably not have lasted for many more years, but since this photograph was taken, the roof has been expertly repaired by the National Park Authority mason.

Removal of old iron fence posts at Redlake

Redlake was an early twentieth-century china clay pit, and when excavation ceased in 1932 the commoners were concerned about the danger of the open pit to their stock. The pit was duly fenced, using as posts steel from the Redlake tramway. By 1985 the wire had long since rotted while the posts still stood as unsightly, rusty and, in their turn, somewhat dangerous stumps in the open moor.

Teams of volunteers spent several days helping the Rangers to dig out or cut off the offending posts. They enjoyed the job, hard work though it was, and, at the end of a day's work, posed for a photograph.

Snow on Pork Hill

During most winters there are few a days when severe drifting on the roads prevents vehicles from passing.

The Duchy of Cornwall estate

Pizwell, seen across the northern end of Cator Common, is one of the ancient tenements – the medieval settlements, often two or three farmsteads together, whose occupants were the first tenants of the Duchy of Cornwall on Dartmoor. Pizwell is first recorded in 1260, so it predates the take-over of the Forest by the Duchy in 1337.

At Pizwell there are three longhouses (see pages 90–91), one still occupied, others now used as farm buildings. Because of the history of the site and its obvious interest, the Duchy of Cornwall, with help from the National Park Authority, has refurbished one shippon, removed modern appendages from another and is renewing slate roofs in the group. The Duchy and the Authority work in partnership in these matters, following guidelines jointly developed, and published in 1983, on the initiative of the Secretary of the Duchy. H.R.H. Prince Charles took an active interest in the process and visited Dartmoor many times between 1981 and 1983 while principles were being hammered out.

The result is an attempt at the reconciliation of the conservation of the quality, interest and accessibility of the landscape and buildings of the estate with the Duchy tenants' entitlement to as good a Dartmoor livelihood as possible. The National Park Authority helps on both counts – with management agreements that conserve landscape features *and* contribute to the income of the holding. It also grant-aids building refurbishment and tree planting on the estate, and carries out some works directly.

The Duchy is the largest landowner in the National Park and its estate includes the heart of the high moorland and almost all of the northern moor, hence the Authority's great interest in the maintenance of this working partnership.

Frozen wool

A passing sheep has left a few strands of wool on the ubiquitous barbed wire strung along walls and hedges to contain the agile Scotch Blackface sheep.

Hazel catkins

The male flowers of many trees take the form of catkins. Hazel catkins appear from mid-January until March. These are the male catkins, bearing flowers with stamens only. The female flowers are small and bud-like with crimson stigmas. Pollen from the catkins fertilizes the female which develops, by autumn, into a cluster of hazel nuts.

Postbridge after a snowfall

In winter this is a scene of black-and-white simplicity, with the medieval clapper bridge spanning the East Dart River at Postbridge, and Bellever Forest stretching across the horizon.

Horse-riding

The open swards of grass and heather make Dartmoor a riders' paradise. There are dangers in places, of course – rough uneven ground and clitter (surface granite boulders) – but moor-wise pony and rider can normally safely pick a way through. There are several riding stables on the moor which offer visitors a choice from a few hours to a whole day on horseback – a most exhilarating experience.

An evening in the pub

The pubs in Dartmoor's towns and villages are a vital part of community life, as they are all over the country. Indeed, the more remote the village, the more valued is the pub as a meeting place and a common ground. Even the tiniest village has its pub. The town of Moretonhampstead, with a population of 1600, comfortably supports five!

Winter sunset

From Merrivale is a beautiful view to the west at a time, as T.S. Eliot said, 'when the evening is spread out against the sky'. The tor is Pew Tor and the distant skyline, bathed in gold, is Cornwall.

An unusual view of Haytor

'Snow had fallen, snow on snow,' and the furze bushes on Haytor Down lie covered by a deep white all-embracing blanket. Only the rocks on the horizon stand out hard and black by contrast. On Dartmoor snow falls each winter on about eighteen days, and normally lies for considerably longer.

National Park Services

The National Park runs seven **Information Centres** which operate during the holiday season. The assistants are knowledgeable local people whose daily fare ranges from holiday-related queries (where can we stay . . . eat . . . walk . . . see a . . . visit a . . .? etc.) to the more demanding enquiries about geology, history, natural history and present-day conservation of Dartmoor. Some questions can be answered in only a few words while others would need a thesis to do them justice!

Most of the Centres are situated around the edge of the Park to assist visitors on their way in. Two only are in the middle – Princetown and Postbridge. They are all fairly small, the main service being the personal attention and advice of a welcoming member of staff.

Apart from those in Tavistock and Okehampton, the Centres are at sites where guided walks start and which in themselves are traditional attractive starting points for visiting the moor – usually beside a river. The photograph shows the Centre at Parke, Bovey Tracey, where the National Park Department has its headquarters.

The main interpretive thrust of the National Park since 1972 has been its **Guided Walks** programme. The Authority believes that the best way to discover Dartmoor is to explore its diversity on foot, accompanied by moor-wise National Park guides who will share their knowledge and love of the moor. From Easter until the end of September there is a walk nearly every day with walks of 1½, 3 and 6 hours from many different starting points.

The programme is printed in full in the annual publication **The Dartmoor Visitor.** This free newspaper also contains details of local events, arts and crafts, camping, riding, fishing, places of interest and entertainment and other useful information.

The National Park's seven Information Centres are open daily from Easter to the end of October, from 10.00 a.m. to 5.00 p.m.

NEWBRIDGE: between Ashburton and Princetown. Riverside car park with toilets. Picnics, strolls, guided walks.

STEPS BRIDGE: near Dunsford in Teign valley. Car park, toilets, hotel. Woodland and riverside strolls and guided walks.

POSTBRIDGE: middle of moor on B3212. Riverside picnics, walking access to the north moor. Guided walks. Slide shows daily.

TAVISTOCK: Town Hall Buildings, Bedford Square, in the centre of this attractive town. Short slide show about Tavistock on request.

OKEHAMPTON: Museum of Dartmoor Life courtyard, adjacent to White Hart Hotel in main street. Displays of aspects of Dartmoor's history and historic reconstructions in the museum.

PRINCETOWN: centre of village. Good point from which to explore the western side of Dartmoor.

PARKE: just outside Bovey Tracey on Haytor/Manaton road. Interpretive Centre. Riverside and woodland walks. Slide shows. Adjacent to Rare Breeds Farm. National Park Headquarters.

For information at all other times send s.a.e. to The Dartmoor National Park Authority, Parke, Bovey Tracey, TQ13 9JQ, or telephone Bovey Tracey (0626) 832093 during office hours.

Watch over the National Parks

There are ten national parks in England and Wales, each run by its own authority. These authorities have worked hard to maintain a balance between the protection of the countryside and the need for employment and services for local communities. However, during the thirty years since the national parks were set up many changes have taken place. Leisure time and mobility have increased and farming methods have altered. Pressure for development in the national parks is unrelenting.

To ensure future protection for the parks we need to be aware of the threats they face. This is why, in 1985, the Countryside Commission, together with the national park authorities and the Council for National Parks, launched a two-year campaign called **Watch over the National Parks**.

The aims of the campaign are:

- to increase public awareness of the national parks, what they have to offer and the ideals and principles which led to their establishment;
- to establish a secure future for the national parks, especially through positive support from central and local government;
- to create an understanding of how the parks are run, and the role and duties of the national park authorities and the Countryside Commission.

New guidebooks and other material provide information for visitors to the national parks, for farmers, landowners, voluntary bodies, commercial interests, local communities and anyone concerned about the future of these special landscapes.

Friends of the National Parks

This membership arm of the Council for National Parks is open to anyone who wishes to support the work of the Council in protecting the national parks. Members are kept informed of issues affecting the parks through the journal *Tarn and Tor*.

The CNP is a voluntary body working on behalf of the ten national parks to safeguard conservation and recreation interests. It campaigns on behalf of national parks, provides educational resources and a lecture service, publishes major reports on such issues as agriculture and military use, defends the parks against specific threats and works to ensure greater public awareness of the parks' value.

Details of membership can be obtained from the Council for National Parks and all national park information centres.

USEFUL ADDRESSES:

Dartmoor National Park Authority, Parke, Haytor Road, Bovey Tracey, Devon TQ13 9JQ
Tel: Bovey Tracey (0626) 832093

Council for National Parks, 45 Shelton Street, London WC2H 9HJ
Tel: 01 240 3603

Countryside Commission, South West Regional Office, Bridge House, Sion Place, Clifton Down, Bristol, BS8 4AS
Tel: Bristol (0272) 739966

Dartmoor Preservation Association, Honorary Secretary, Crossings Cottage, Dousland, Yelverton, Devon.

Devon Trust for Nature Conservation, 35 New Bridge Street, Exeter, Devon EX4 3AH
Tel: Exeter (0392) 79244

Duchy of Cornwall, Bowhill, Bradninch, Exeter EX5 4LH
Tel: Exeter (0392) 881210

Forestry Commission, Bullers Hill, Kennford, Exeter EX6 7XR
Tel: Exeter (0392) 832262

National Trust, Devon Regional Office, Killerton House, Broadclyst, Exeter, Devon EX5 3LE
Tel: Exeter (0392) 881691

South West Water, Peninsula House, Rydon Lane, Exeter, Devon EX2 7HR
Tel: Exeter (0392) 219666

West Country Tourist Board, Trinity Court, Southernhay East, Exeter, Devon EX1 1QS
Tel: Exeter (0392) 76351

Other information

WEATHER:

Local numbers for recorded forecasts based on Meteorological Office information: Exeter: (0392) 8091; Torquay (0803) 8091; Plymouth (0752) 8091.

FIRING RANGES:

The Ministry of Defence has a large training area on the northern part of Dartmoor. Access is prohibited during firing; times of firing are advertised in local newspapers every Friday and notices are displayed in local police stations, post offices and some inns. There is also a telephone answering service on the following numbers: Torquay: (0803) 24592; Exeter (0392) 70164; Plymouth (0752) 701924; Okehampton (0837) 2939.

RESCUE:

In case of emergency on the moor or genuine cause for concern dial 999 for the Police who will alert the Dartmoor Rescue Group.

PUBLIC RIGHTS OF WAY:

Footpaths are marked by yellow waymarkers (round dots) and bridlepaths by blue ones.

DRIVING AND PARKING:

Take care of the moorland stock when driving over the moor. Many accidents each year cause pain and death to ponies, sheep and cattle.

It is illegal to drive more than 15 yards from the road on to the common.

CAMPING:

A list of camp sites is published in the annual *Dartmoor Visitor*. Elsewhere, on enclosed land the permission of the owner must be sought. On open moor a single tent may usually be pitched out of sight of roads or houses, but if asked to move on, you must comply.

FISHING:

Before fishing you must have a current South West Water Rod Licence and a permit from the landowner. Both can be obtained from distributors at many places on the moor (see *Dartmoor Visitor* for list).

River fishing (salmon and trout) is available on the Dart, Tavy, Walkham, Plym, Meavy and Teign. Reservoir fishing is available at the Avon Reservoir, Meldon, Venford, Burrator, Fernworthy, Kennick and Tottiford. At the last four, licences (including permit) are available on site.